LAUGHTE

Laughter
In Heaven

The Christian Message
Through Drama

Edited by

MURRAY WATTS

KINGSWAY PUBLICATIONS
EASTBOURNE

ISBN 0 85476 520 4

Produced by Bookprint Creative Services
P.O. Box 827, BN21 3YJ, England for
KINGSWAY PUBLICATIONS
Lottbridge Drove, Eastbourne, E. Sussex BN23 6NT.
Printed in Great Britain

Foreword

'In my mind, there is nothing so illiberal and so ill-bred, as audible laughter.' So wrote an eighteenth-century aristocrat, who also held the opinion that: 'Religion is by no means a proper subject of conversation in a mixed company.' Since laughter and religion were equally a source of embarrassment to the unfortunate earl, one wonders what he would have made of religious jokes. 'I say, my lord, did you ever hear the one about the vicar and the parrot?' Clearly, this would not have been the best opening gambit for a potential son-in-law. As for producing a book called *Laughter in Heaven*, I suppose this would have excluded the authors from polite society for ever.

There have been others down the centuries, who – whilst not sharing the earl's inhibition about discussing religion – have frowned upon humour, especially in church. The authors of these sketches have occasionally received letters of complaint. One which I received argued that truth and humour could never be mixed, because the humour would be remembered and the truth forgotten; another, that humour 'destroys the very heart of the gospel'. Needless to say, I disagree. In fact, I believe quite the reverse. The Resurrection is the greatest happy ending to a story that the world has ever known. It turned the sorrow of the disciples into joy. Today, it can turn the bitterest of our tears into laughter.

Laughter liberates. It sets us free from self-obsession, the worst form of human bondage. It brings perspective. Taking ourselves too seriously encourages pride and erects barriers between Christians; when the church takes itself too seriously, it becomes an impenetrable wall between the world and God. Laughter breaks that wall down. It brings men and women into a fellowship which is, essentially, a recognition of need for God. We can laugh together, without being threatened, at the absurdity of our own actions; laughter becomes an open window, through which the truth can pierce the soul.

There may be no place in the church for the hollow laughter of mockery and unbelief; but there is no place for a church which never resounds with the laughter of faith. Such a church commits a crime against humanity: it has become boring.

There are many serious obstacles to spreading the gospel, but this is one of the worst. It is no good blaming the world for being blind to the truth, when we are blind to it ourselves. If we are not free, how can we liberate others? If we are not faithful to the uniqueness of the Resurrection experience, to the delight and heavenly joy which is ours for eternity, if we are dull, we short-change our fellow men. We give them our narrow piety, instead of Christ. There is nothing more interesting than the Christian gospel, more profound, more extraordinary and more exciting. Nothing can ever rival that historic event, which turned the world upside down. The laughter born on that Easter morning is a gift from heaven, which draws us closer to that day, when 'God will wipe every tear from our eyes, and death shall be no more, neither shall there be mourning nor crying nor pain any more, for the former things have passed away '

Murray Watts
YORK,
APRIL, 1985

Licences to perform the sketches in this volume

ACKNOWLEDGEMENTS

Buzz Magazine for permission to reprint *One in a Million* and *Final Resolution*; Hodder and Stoughton for permission to reprint *General Conformity*, a scene from *The Trial of Trimmer Trend* first published separately as a sketch in *Lightning Sketches*.

INTRODUCTION

Five authors have contributed fifteen sketches and a morality play to produce this book. The main characteristic of the material – bringing together many different styles – is comedy. There are one or two exceptions to this rule. *A Man After My Own*, by Nigel Forde, is more an ironic comment on a tragic situation than a funny sketch; it illustrates how easily we deceive ourselves into adultery. An audience may smile, as it recognises its own image, but it is just as likely to shed a tear. *Do unto Others ...*, by Paul Burbridge, in which people cannot face up to the suffering of others, is both ridiculous and sad. Yet, for the most part, there is a clear vein of comedy running through *Laughter in Heaven*, ranging from the broad, in *Quick Quaker* and *Bodyguard*, to the subtle in *Lexicon*.

The writers share faith in Christ. They also share a love of laughter. There are other factors uniting the writers, principally friendship and some relationship with Riding Lights Theatre Company. Paul Burbridge is Artistic Director, Nigel Forde and I are Associate Directors; Richard Everett has served as a trustee of the Riding Lights Trust, and contributed as a playwright; Andrew Goreing has lived in York and worked with the company, writing a play and several sketches. All the same, this is not, strictly speaking, a manual of Riding Lights sketches. (Richard Everett's, for instance, have never been performed by the company.) Rather, this is a personal anthology, chosen and edited by myself, of material that I felt would be serviceable to churches looking for fresh inspiration, either using drama in evangelism, worship or simply – quite justifiably – for fun.

The sketches could have been divided into sections. For instance, *Bodyguard*, *100% Proof*, *Quick Quaker*, *Jonah's Journey*, *The Interrogation* and *Using Your Loaf*, are all biblical sketches; whereas, *A Dig at the Twentieth Century*, *A Man After My Own*, *Do unto Others ...*, *Lexicon*, and *Service with a Smile* are all satirical sketches, which take a look at modern attitudes; and the remaining four, *One in a Million*, *Final Resolution*, *Talking Heads* and *Life Is But a Melancholy Flower*, all have something to say about what it means to be a Christian. Yet these categories are artificial: the Bible has as much to do with the modern world as it has with the ancient; there is an element of satire in much of the material; and any of the truths expressed in this book tell us something about what it means to be a Christian. So instead, the material is presented simply as an anthology, arranged for variety but with no particular theme in mind. Each sketch has its own introduction, written by the author, and can be looked at quite independently of the others. The type of introduction has been left to individual discretion. The sketches speak for themselves, and some introductions are a stimulus to thought and to new writers, rather than an essential briefing for performance.

Laughter in Heaven is a resource book of different kinds of material, needing the right context for performance. Careful study of the sketches should make this plain. Some sketches, like *Bodyguard*, will obviously work as street theatre; *The Trial of Trimmer Trend* can be performed as a street theatre play; but other material is more suitable for church services, student audiences, and so on. Again, it is idle to attempt a classification here, because most sketches will work in several situations. A quick glance at the contents will show that over half the sketches have been written by Nigel Forde, for many years the mastermind behind the award-winning revues presented by Riding Lights at the Edinburgh Festival. *Lexicon* and *A Dig at the Twentieth Century* are two of Nigel's most popular revue sketches. Literary wit, satire and an off-beat sense of humour have been the hallmark of his sketches, whether based on the Bible or on his own observations of life. This kind of material will frequently work well in a student context or where an audience enjoys a sophisticated sense of humour; *Lexicon* is obviously not a street theatre sketch. Longer, more subtle sketches require, at the very least, a consistent audience and reasonable quiet. *Bodyguard* and *Quick Quaker* are a better choice for a youth club with a disco thumping in the background. Richard Everett's sketch *One in a Million*, written for *Buzz Magazine*, is a very different type of sketch from many of the others: for instance, a character called 'Bobby Gobstopper' appears dressed as a boiled sweet. This cartoon style is discussed in the article on morality plays. As a TV quiz show, the sketch is best performed with good costumes and effects. It is very visual, and will work according to how accurately the style is parodied. Sketches like this, that pick up on our TV culture, are extremely useful in communicating to a generation of TV addicts.

The Trial of Trimmer Trend is a full-length morality play, which I originally wrote for Breadrock Street Theatre Company. I have provided some background to morality plays, in the hope that this will reawaken interest in a fascinating type of Christian communication; and I have also given a detailed introduction to producing the play, which is a much more demanding enterprise than performing a sketch in a church service.

One final word: I hope that this book will make enjoyable reading, but it is not intended for armchair enthusiasts. There is as much difference between reading this book and performing the material, as there is between studying a musical score and playing in a concert. This is live entertainment; so let it live!

Other Books by the Riding Lights Theatre Company

TIME TO ACT   Paul Burbridge and Murray Watts (Hodder and Stoughton)

LIGHTNING SKETCHES   Paul Burbridge and Murray Watts (Hodder and Stoughton)

Contents

SKETCHES

Bodyguard
by Andrew Goreing

COMMANDING OFFICER SERGEANT-MAJOR SOLDIER ONE
SOLDIER TWO

This sketch does not attempt to harmonise the various Gospel accounts of the Resurrection. It is not an exploration of the militaristic mind. It is not an accurate record of social life in the Roman legions. The joy of Easter, though, may have room for a bit of fun, and this should be fun. If it isn't, you can't be doing it right.

The Commanding Officer's office, the C.O. *behind his desk. The* SERGEANT-MAJOR (RSM) *marches in two soldiers.*

RSM:	*(Klaxon-voiced throughout)* By the left, quick march hup two three, up two three, cummanee, halt! A-ten-shun!
C.O.:	What's going on, sarnt-major?
RSM:	Two men on report, sah. Come on straighten up you two, straighten up that line!
SOLDIER ONE:	Does he have to shout so loud?
RSM:	I don't want any lip from you, you disgusting little vermin!
C.O.:	Yes, thank you, sarnt-major, I'll deal with this …
ONE:	I want my mum … *(sob)*
RSM:	I'm your mother now, sunshine!
C.O.:	Yes, very maternal, sarnt-major, very good. Now, what are you men on report for, eh?
RSM:	Total and enormous incompetence sah!
C.O.:	Oh dear, we can't have that, can we? You see, you chaps, you're in the Roman Army now.
SOLDIER TWO:	Yes sir.
RSM:	What are you in, you filth?
ONE:	Roman Army sarge.

RSM: What happens to be – ?

ONE: Best army in the world sarge.

RSM: Until?

ONE: Until us disgusting little vermin joined up sarge. (*Sob, sniff*)

C.O.: Thank you, sarnt-major, your tact is legendary. Now, you men, what exactly have you been up to, hm?

TWO: Sir, we let a prisoner escape, sir.

C.O.: That really won't do, you know. He wasn't too much of a trouble-maker, I hope.

TWO: We didn't think he'd cause much trouble no, sir.

C.O.: And why was that?

TWO: He was a little tied up, sir.

C.O.: Good, yes, we do encourage you to tie prisoners up from time to time.

TWO: Well, he was more than tied up, sir, as a matter of fact –

ONE: He was dead. (*Sniff, sob*)

C.O.: Sorry, didn't catch that …

RSM: He was dead, sah!!

C.O.: Yes, I caught that, sarnt-major … so what we have is a dead, tied-up prisoner, who's managed to escape Clever fellow, what?

TWO: Yes sir.

C.O.: You do seem to have been more than a little negligent.

TWO: Yes sir, very sorry sir.

RSM: Apologise to the C.O.!

ONE: It's not fair, it wasn't our fault, honest sir …

RSM: Silence!! Crying is not allowed in the Roman Army!

ONE: Can't have any fun in the Roman Army .

C.O.: Let's get to the bottom of this, shall we? Who was this deceased escapee?

TWO: Jesus-bar-Joseph, sir. Itinerant preacher from Galilee. Thought to have zealot sympathies, sir.

C.O.: I see.

TWO: Sanhedrin demanded his arrest, sir.

C.O.: Ah-ha …

TWO: Last Thursday, sir.

C.O.: On what charge?

TWO: Claiming to be God sir.

TWO: Claiming to be God, sir.

C.O.: Claiming to be whom?

RSM: God, sah, spelt G – O – D.

C.O.: Thank you, sarnt-major, I know how to spell God ... Died in custody, eh?

TWO: Crucified on Friday, sir.

C.O.: I see.

TWO: And then buried, sir.

C.O.: Uh-hum.

TWO: Then he ... went, sir.

C.O.: Went? (RSM *opens his mouth*) Thank you, sarnt-major, I know what 'went' means. Could you elaborate, soldier?

TWO: Tomb's empty, body's gone.

C.O.: Ah.

ONE: And people are saying he's alive. Ow! (*as* RSM *clips him round the ear*)

C.O.: Well, it sounds to me as if the whole business has been messed up from start to finish. What idiot was in charge of the execution?

RSM: You were, sah.

C.O.: I was? Impossible.

RSM: Distinctly remember, sah.

C.O.: (*Looking in his diary*) Perhaps it is just possible. Well, they were dead, all three of 'em, poor blighters.

TWO: Sir.

C.O.: So what did you do with the body?

TWO: Buried it sir.

C.O.: Good ... where?

TWO: Tomb carved out of the rock, sir.

C.O.: Properly sealed?

TWO: The door was secure, sir.

ONE: Door? Door? It was a bl— a whopping great rock! Ouch!

RSM: Vermin, how dare you use language to your commanding officer.

C.O.: Thank you, sarnt-major, so glad you're concerned with my moral welfare.

RSM: Pleasure, sah.

C.O.: Carry on, soldier.

TWO: We guarded the tomb, sir.

C.O.: Why was that?

TWO: The chief priests asked for a guard of regular soldiers, sir.

RSM: Beats me why on earth they picked these

two, sorry sah.

TWO: This character had been in the way of making threats, sir, namely that in three days he would rise from the dead.

RSM: This situation is not catered for in army regulations sah.

C.O.: You surprise me, sarnt-major.

TWO: It was feared that some of Jesus-bar-Joseph's followers would attempt to purloin the body, sir. We were to foil any such attempt.

C.O.: So? What happened?

TWO: Well, I …

ONE: There was an angel!

TWO: Earth tremors …

ONE: The stone just rolled away …

TWO: A dazzling light …

ONE: It gives you the hab-dabs …

TWO: We were briefly stunned, sir. And the tomb was definitely empty. The body had gone.

ONE: And the chief priests gave us some money … (*He is muffled by* SOLDIER TWO)

C.O.: What's that?

RSM: What's that what's that what's that?

TWO: Nothing sarge, slip of the tongue.

C.O.: No, no, let him alone; come on, man, out with it.

ONE: Sir the chief priests sir when we said what had happened sir, they gave us some money sir to put the word around sir, that Jesus's followers had been and stolen the body while we were asleep. Sir.

C.O.: What a very good story. Eh, sarnt-major?

ONE: Yes, isn't it?

C.O.: Look, you silly man, in the first place, if you were asleep you wouldn't know what was going on anyway; and in the second place, if you were asleep on guard duty you've earned yourself three weeks in the glasshouse.

ONE: Oh sir. (*Crumpling into tears again*)

C.O.: Now now, pull yourself together … can't bear seeing grown men cry …

RSM: Right shower, this lot, sir, give 'em a proper flogging, I would sah.

TWO: With respect sir –

ONE: It's not fair, sir, it's not, he did come back to

life, dozens and dozens of people have seen him they say and I don't think it's natural …

C.O.: Yes yes, very well, I tell you what; if you hand over the money you received into my safekeeping, then I might just be persuaded to forget the whole incident, what?

ONE: Persuade him, persuade him …

TWO: (*Handing over some notes*) With our compliments, sir.

C.O.: Why, how very generous of you … send them away, sarnt-major.

RSM: (*Very suspicious of this deal*) Very well sah. Right you lot, hop it, at the double, count yourselves lucky I'm not in charge of you … (*The soldiers depart*)

C.O.: Oh, and sarnt-major …

RSM: Yes sah?

C.O.: (*Peeling him off a note from the wad*) Be a good chap, don't mention this business to anyone, will you?

RSM: No sah, thank you sah …

C.O.: Extraordinary story, what? And people claiming to have seen this fellow since he um er …

RSM: Yes sah, highly strornery, most peculiar sah.

C.O.: What do you think of it, sarnt-major?

RSM: *Me* sah? *Think*, sah?

C.O.: No, never mind, sarnt-major

(*Blackout*)

100% PROOF
By Nigel Forde

After seeing the Riding Lights' production of 'St. John's Gospel', a member of the audience was heard to remark, 'The Resurrection was incredible!'. Of the same sort is the remark with which I was going to open this introduction: miracles are very hard to perform on stage. Hourly I expect a call from the editor of the Penguin Dictionary of Truisms.

But you know what I mean. How do you begin to show a miracle in sketch form? The short answer is that you don't: you show, instead, the effect of that miracle. You let your imagination play over the sort of people who might have been around when the miracle happened; what did they see? What did they think? How were their attitudes to Jesus changed? After all, the miracle itself, even if we could find a way of enacting it, would have no significance: its power lies in the way it affected those who experienced it.

The sketch itself is not a complicated one. Its main difficulty lies in combining a sufficiently realistic telephone technique with the realisation that the audience must not feel excluded. If HYMIE *is played as a very confident and perhaps slightly too clever wide-boy, his open physical attitude even while on the telephone will dispose of most of the problem.*

A telephone on a table with a chair beside it, downstage left of centre. The wedding is going on way beyond the downstage right corner of the stage, far enough distant for HYMIE *to be private, but not so distant that he can't see what is going on.* HYMIE *enters, slipping away from his responsibilities for a quick, illegal phone call. He treads on the butt of the cigarette he should not have been smoking, puts down the half-finished glass of wine which he considers himself entitled to and dials. While Jewish Telecom are performing electronic miracles he watches the wedding with an indulgent but professional smile. At last he is through.*

> HYMIE: Ah, hello? John? John?? John! Hello! ...
> Hymie here! ... Hymie – from Cana Catering
> ... Hello! Now, listen, John – I've got some
> great material for you for chapter two ... Yes,
> he's here! At the wedding. Yes, it says on the
> guest-list ... Well, not actually 'Jesus', no: it
> says 'Yeshua bar Yosef and Party', but it must

be the same one! (*John is describing Jesus at the other end of the phone.* HYMIE *is checking off the features and gesturing at his own face*) Yeah, that's right … with a … yeah … and long … just round the … yeah! He's having a great time! … He's brought his mum! … No, course he's not, John! He's not even tiddly. Coo, you must be jokin' – at a Kosher wedding? We'll be lucky if there's enough for two glasses each! (*He quickly finishes off what is left in his own glass*) Oh, it's the usual story, John: more trouble in the vineyard; labour relations. (*He makes a 'so-so' gesture with his free hand, fingers outspread like a pianist playing octaves on an imaginary piano*) Look, look, look, look!! (*Jesus has just done something particularly delightful and* HYMIE *holds out the phone so that John can see. Then he realises …*) Sorry, John. Look, are you sure he's – you know, who you say he is? Yeah? … Yeah … Yeah … Well, he's not your average Messiah, is he? I mean, he's been chattin' to Lebanon Lil for the past half hour … yeah, I dunno what he said but she has been unusually restrained … no argy-bargy at all! And he's been laughing and joking with young Barnabas – the wine-waiter … yeah, common as dirt, but it doesn't seem to worry him! … Look, no offence, John. I know you're a clever lad an' all that, but I don't think he can be the … well, you know – who you say he is … Well because he's so normal, you know, ordinary, friendly. Now he couldn't be like that if he was the Son of … you know … (*Slightly impatient at John's confidence*) All right then, John, why isn't he sitting up at the top table with all the big nobs then, eh? (*Suddenly furtive and quiet*) Look, don't quote me on this, John, but I wish he *was* the Messiah; he's the sort of bloke you could really get on with, know what I mean? … Well, I don't know that I *can* explain it, really … (*Then he thinks of a way*) Look, you know when you told me he was … well, when you told me who he was? I thought 'Coo!

Famous, eh? I'll have to have a word!' Just to
say, you know ... (*He is slightly embarrassed
at admitting his admiration of the famous*)
Only when I did speak to him, he was just
like me. (*Suddenly shocked at what he has
just implied*) No, that sounds awful; I didn't
mean *that*, John ... I mean he was like I
would have been ... wanted to be ... when I
wanted ... *if* I'd been ... had I not turned out
to be ... when ... know what I mean, John?
Hang on just a sec. (*He shouts offstage left to
a waiter*) Barnabas! Almost time for the
speeches! Better bring out a case of the
Kishon Rosé and the Chateau Bethany '22.
(*Back to the phone*) Sorry, John; you were
saying? ... Anything happened? What do
you mean 'anything'? ... Ah! Well! Yes! A
couple of ... I don't know what you'd call
them really: miracles, I suppose ... Well, for
a start, the bride's mother has smiled ...
Twice ... *And* she's actually spoken to the
groom's mother. (*Nods into the phone*)
Yeah, well you might not, John, and it might
not be big enough to put into chapter two,
but *I'd* say it was a miracle, and if you knew
the bride's mother like I know the ... (*He is
apparently interrupted from offstage left*)
What? ... Yes it *is* ... Look, I won't swear to
the Rosé, but there are two cases of Chateau
Bethany and one of Veuve de Tekoa on the
left in the cellar. (*Back to phone, with a
pitying laugh at Barnabas's stupidity*) Sorry
about that, John; it's the casual staff –
thought all the wine had gone! Now, what
were we talking about? Oh, yes – miracles.
You see, John, I haven't had much experience of miracles – not in the normal course of
things. No ... no, no – I'd say I was as open-
minded as anybody else in this day and age,
but you've got to keep your feet on the
ground, haven't you, John? (*Barnabas is
presumed to pass in front of him, at a little
distance.* HYMIE *sees what he is carrying and
panics*) Barnabas? Barnabas!! Where are
you going with that! You can't serve *that*!

That's not wine, you fool, it's only water!
Barnabas!!! (*Back to phone. His voice is low
and desperate*) John. Look. We got a bit of a
panic on here. It seems the wine *has* run out
and some idiot has hit on the idea of serving
up bath water! (*Drops phone and stands to
speak to Barnabas. He tries to shout in a
whisper*) Barnabas! No! You can't *do* that,
Barnabas! I ... I don't care *who* told you to
bring it. *Who* told you to bring it??? Barnabas! (*Picks up phone*) John! (*Towards
wedding party*) Barnabas! (*For a second he
gets slightly confused between the two*) Bar-
nab ... er ... John, John, he's done it! (*Covers
his eyes so that he cannot see the awful
moment. Then he opens his fingers and peeps
through: he has to look*) And they're drinking
it!! Oh, the shame! The i-gonomy of it! And
with *Him* here as well! Ohhhhh ... I shall
never be asked to do another function as
long as I live! No no no, don't go now John;
I need you! (*To Barnabas, who has returned
to offstage left*) Here, Barnabas! Give us a
glass of that water! (*He hands his glass
offstage and it is filled with wine.* HYMIE *is too
miserable to watch what is going on. He
brings the glass back, sits down, picks up the
phone again, takes a sip. Freezes. Drops
phone into his lap. Looks at glass. Takes
another sip, rolls it round his mouth à la
wine-taster and places the glass carefully and
wonderingly on the table. Turns slowly to
look offstage*) Barnabas ... I thought you ...
how did the ... is this what ... ? (*Gathers his
thoughts and speaks clearly and precisely*)
Barnabas, how much of this have we got? ...
(*Nods slowly*) ... about 180 gallons ... (*Very
deliberately drinks his wineglass dry*) Now,
John. Miracles. Yes. Look, John, I don't
want to be categorical about it; all I'm saying
is, I'd need some pretty convincing proof.
After all, I'm not an unreasonable bloke; it's
just that you've got to keep your head
screwed on, haven't you, John ... ?

(*Lights fade to blackout*)

Quick Quaker or Paul and Silas do Porridge in Philippi
by Paul Burbridge

NARRATOR ONE   NARRATOR TWO   *A group of three or more actors who take the various parts, including:*   THE JAILER   PAUL   SILAS

This sketch develops the reliable format of two narrators plus accompanying mime, by giving much of the dialogue to the actors. The director will need to decide how far to illustrate the narrated sequences with action on stage. The narrators should be in control and maintain a fast-moving pace. There is an obvious cartoon element to this piece and any props and costumes should reflect this.

The story of the Philippian Jailer can teach us many things, not least the power of prayer and praise in the midst of crises and the way in which 'all things work together for good for those who love God'.

ONE: Come with us now on a journey down Memory Lane.

TWO: Ding! Ding! Fares please. Brrrmmmm ...

ONE: And stop.

TWO: (*FX: Screech*)

ONE: At the first century ad.

ACTOR A: (*Leaping on, speaking at the racy tempo of a TV advert*) Hi! My name's Quintus Plutonius. I'm a general in the Roman Army. Many of my men suffer from dandruff. (*Produces large meat cleaver*) I use 'Head and Shoulders'. No one's ever been back to complain.

TWO: Excuse me. The script is actually referring to the first century A.D.

ONE: Not the first century ad.

ACTOR A: (*Miffed*) Oh. (*Suddenly to the audience*) Well, while I'm here, have you tried 'NEW, JELLY-MEAT CHRISTIANS!' My lions love 'em. (*He brandishes a tin*)

TWO: No, thank you.

ONE: Would you go, please.

TWO: Now. (*Exit* ACTOR A, *muttering about rich*

gravy sauce)

ONE: (*Recovering composure*) In the first century

TWO: Life was tough.

ONE: (*FX: Crunch*)

TWO: And men were wild.

ACTOR B: (*Crossing stage hurriedly, dressed as a hippy*) Wow! Far out, man. (*Exit*)

ONE: Watch closely as we enter the little old seaside town of

TWO: Philippi.

ONE: A throbbing metropolis.

TWO: Throb-throb, throb-throb.

ONE: Under the hot Macedonian sun,

TWO: (*Sharp intake of breath*)

ONE: Cooled only by the merest breath

TWO: (*Little sigh*)

ONE: (*With fierce look at* TWO) Of Mediterranean wind,

TWO: (*Burp*)

ONE: Thank you! Nestles Philippi

TWO: As it has done for centuries

ONE: Beneath the rugged hills

TWO: Betwixt the ribbed slopes

ONE: Beside the ragged sea.

ACTOR A: (*Entering from upstage*) Look, would you mind pushing this along a bit, please?

ONE: (*Defensively*) We were just setting the scene

TWO: For the story about the Philippian Jailer.

ONE: (*To* ACTOR A) Here, go on, you be the Philippian Jailer.

ACTOR A: I don't want to be the flippin' jailer!

TWO: *Philippian* Jailer.

ACTOR A: Don't want to be him, either.

ONE: Helmet. (*Appropriate props and costumes are thrust upon him*)

TWO: Sword

ONE: Silly Roman Jailer's costume.

TWO: Keys.

ONE: Truncheon.

ACTOR A: Feel stupid.

TWO: (*Pleased that they can now get on with it*) Good.

ONE: Every day

TWO: The jailer went cheerfully about his business:

ONE: Arresting people

TWO: Having them flogged

ONE: Locking them up

TWO: (*Getting carried away*) Thumbscrews! The rack! I'm sorry.

ONE: And putting their feet in the stocks.

TWO: Because there weren't any chairs. (*Explaining his little joke*) Stocks and chairs. Sorry.

ONE: Now it was the jailer's job to see that everything remained nice and quiet.

TWO: In this nice, quiet, little town. (*Total uproar offstage*)

ONE: Uh-oh, a spot of provocation in the marketplace.

TWO: (*In the kind of American accent used for Walt Disney animal films*) It's not yet coffee-time and he's landed himself in a whole heap o' trouble.

ONE: Immediately he's at the scene of the crime.

TWO: (*FX: Batman zoom*)

JAILER: (*Re-entering*) Now then, now then. What's all this 'ere?

ONE: But, of course, being a Roman policeman he speaks in Latin.

JAILER: Nunc tunc, nunc tunc. Quid omnis hic hoc?

TWO: And right in the middle of it all were

ONE: You guessed

TWO: Two Christians.

ONE: Our old friends, Paul

TWO: And Silas. (*Two actors rush on eagerly*)

ACTOR B: I'll be Paul!

ACTOR C: (*Pipped at the post for the best part yet again*) I'll be … Silas.

JAILER: Silas, in court.

SILAS: What for?

JAILER: (*Apprehending him*) Caught yer.

PAUL: You're an unfair cop.

ONE: Said Paul.

SILAS: Why the fuzz?

TWO: Said Silas.

ONE: And other unhelpful remarks.

JAILER: You're breaching the peace, laddie. People tell me you're disturbing our nice, quiet, little town, advocating customs which it is not lawful for us Romans to accept or practise.

TWO: This, of course, was total rubbish.

JAILER: This, of course, is total rubbish. (*He coughs and recovers*) I must warn you that anything you say will be taken down and used in evidence against you. Do you have anything to say?

PAUL: God loves me and Jesus died for my sins.

JAILER: (*Writing ponderously*) God loves me and Jesus died for my – (*realising what he's writing*) All right, that'll do. Come along, lad. (*He marches them offstage*)

ONE: Paul and Silas had only been going about their daily business,

TWO: As servants of the Most High God,

ONE: Healing people

TWO: Exposing racketeers

ONE: And preaching the gospel of salvation.

TWO: The whole charge was trumped up.

ONE: (*FX: Fanfare*)

TWO: Victims of crowd hysteria

ONE: And a downright malicious plot

TWO: They were taken in. (*Enter* JAILER, PAUL *and* SILAS)

SILAS: Hey, we've been taken in!

PAUL: Ssshh!

ONE: Having beaten them with rods

TWO: And torn their clothes

ONE: The magistrates broadmindedly threw them into prison,

TWO: Charging the jailer to keep them safely.

ONE: 'That'll be six pound forty-nine, please.'

TWO: He put them in the inner prison

ONE: Fastened their feet in the stocks

TWO: And went to bed. (*Exit* JAILER)

ONE: Down in the prison

TWO: It was dark. (*The narrators throw blindfolds to* PAUL *and* SILAS)

PAUL: (*After a pause*) Silas!

SILAS: (*Puzzled*) Didn't say a word.

PAUL: You still there?

SILAS: Yeah. Are you?

PAUL: Yeah. While stocks last. Ha, ha, ha. I say, I said while stocks …

SILAS: That's not funny.

PAUL: Sorry.

SILAS: Been inside much, have you?

PAUL: In and out. The Lord looks after me.

SILAS: (*Nervously*) He'll get us out this time, won't he, Paul?

PAUL: (*Smiling*) I was just having a little pray about that.

ONE & TWO: (*FX: Earthquake rumbling.* PAUL *and* SILAS *are jolted*)

SILAS: (*Panic*) WHASSAT!!??

PAUL: Point nine. Closing.

SILAS: What are you talking about?

PAUL: Seismometer.

SILAS: What?

PAUL: It's from the Greek. Seismos. Earthquake.

SILAS: (*Relieved*) Oh, I thought it was my bowels.

ONE: And so, thus comforting themselves,

TWO: Paul and Silas

ONE: Spent the night praying to God and singing.

ACTORS: You didn't tell us we had to sing! I thought this was a theatre company.

TWO: Come on. Chop, chop. Singing.

ACTORS: (*Singing*) Raindrops keep falling on my head.

ONE: Hymns!

ACTORS: (*As a dreadful dirge*) The Church's one foundation is –

TWO: Joyful hymns!

ACTORS: Oh. (*Suddenly with great gusto*)
    Blessings abound where'er he reigns,
    The prisoner leaps to lose his chains,
    (*Brief pause*)
    The weary find eternal rest
    And all the sons of want are blest.

ONE: (*Over the last two lines*) So they sang

TWO: And they sang

ONE: The other prisoners listened to them – amazed.

VOICES: (*Off*) SHUT UUUP! Leave it out, will yer? No, you shut up, I'm listening. I've got a headache.

TWO: And then,

ONE: At about midnight

TWO: Cracks appeared in the ceiling

ONE: Boulders fell from the roof

ONE: Doors were flung open

ONE: The foundations of the prison were shaken

TWO: And everyone's chains were unfastened.
(*Exeunt* PAUL *and* SILAS)

VOICE: (*Off*) Cor! That bloke Paul's got a voice and a half, hasn't he?

ONE: The jailer woke up.

JAILER: (*Rushing on*) Salve, salve, salve?

TWO: 'Allo, 'allo, 'allo?

JAILER: Quid accidit 'ere, then? Who's been re-arranging the floor? A very serious offence, laddie. Breachin' the walls. Do you know what this means?

ONE: The doors are open.

JAILER: Precisely. (*The truth dawns on him*) So they are! Oh, my God!

TWO: Precisely.

JAILER: (*More than a little flustered*) Oh, Zeus! Oh, Hermes! Oh – flippin' 'eck! (*Talking to himself*) Thinks. The doors are open. What would you do then, Watson? Put yourself in their sandals. (*Pacing up and down*) Sandals, sandals. No, you fool. The doors are open, therefore the doors are unlocked. The doors are unlocked therefore the doors are open. So. If I was a prisoner I'd be nippin' off, sharpish. Right. I must kill myself … sharpish. Sword. (*He draws it*) Right, sharpish.

PAUL: (*His head appears*) Careful!

JAILER: Yes. Kill! Kill!

SILAS: Stop! We're all here!

JAILER: (*His sword poised over his stomach*) Stop! We're all – What do you mean we're all here? (*Sees them both behind him*) Ah. 'Evenin' all. (*Catches sight of the sword facing him. He swoons.*)

ONE: It was a nasty shock.

TWO: And for the prison.

PAUL: (*Helping the* JAILER *to his feet*) Here you are.

SILAS: (*Pouring a cup of tea from a Thermos*) It's good for the nerves.

PAUL: (*To* SILAS) What's that, then?

SILAS: Thermos. It's from the Greek.

JAILER: (*Wanly sipping his tea*) Look, Paul and er …

PAUL: (*Filling in*) Silas.

SILAS: (*Mildly indignant*) I didn't say anything.

JAILER: This God of yours ...

PAUL: Yes?

JAILER: Well, um, how can I be saved?

PAUL: Believe in the Lord Jesus Christ.

JAILER: Thanks. I will. (PAUL *and* SILAS *explain the gospel to him as the narrators continue*)

ONE: How's that for a little on-the-spot evangelism?

TWO: Not only did Paul and Silas rejoice with the jailer and his family in their new-found faith,

ONE: They also rejoiced in a hot bath and a slap-up meal.

TWO: At government expense.

ONE: The magistrates came round to apologise for any inconvenience ...

TWO: Such as the flogging ...

ONE: Or ripping their clothes ...

TWO: It was all rather embarrassing, really.

ONE: But Paul and Silas were released.

TWO: So was the jailer ...

ONE: In a way. (*The actors freeze. Blackout*)

Alternatively, for those audiences who might remember Jack Warner in the famous television series 'Dixon of Dock Green', this little epilogue can be used.

(*Enter* SERGEANT DIXON *in policeman's helmet. The other actors hum the familiar theme tune behind him as he takes up his stance, centre stage. He has a sincere and avuncular way of communicating the banal. He smiles.*)

DIXON: You know, earthquakes can be very upsetting at times. (*Pause*) Now, there are big fish and little fish and it's not easy to tell the difference. It all depends on the size. Luckily for the Philippian jailer he was only a little fish in a small prison. (*He hesitates*) But look who got caught in the end? And Paul and Silas? Well, they were the other two characters in the story. So, remember, when you're in some kind of trouble, praising the Lord is the first step to finding a way out. And if you're wondering why I'm going on like this, it's all a question of whether you want your

stories, like fish, open or wrapped. I prefer
mine wrapped. 'Night all. (*He makes a
confident exit.*)

A Dig at the Twentieth Century
by Nigel Forde

PROFESSOR   INTERVIEWER

Swift's satirical method in Gulliver's Travels *remains one of the best: every new civilisation with which Gulliver comes in contact is described and explained. The follies and vices of his own society became clear simply by an implicit comparison with those he encounters.*

A similar method is employed in this sketch; the objectivity is given by the lack of understanding of the twentieth century which is displayed by the two characters involved. Indeed, the method of writing employed was simply to take some contemporary artefacts and to imagine what a mind from an ideal future would make of them. Thus, the tone of the sketch should be one of engrossed fascination; the normal tone, in fact, of the earnest historical documentary with which we are all familiar.

The production of each new object by the PROFESSOR *becomes an enjoyable moment of anticipation by the audience and so, to safeguard this enjoyment, each exhibit should remain hidden in a large hold-all or similar container until it is needed. In a sketch of this length it becomes important that the* PROFESSOR *and the* INTER-VIEWER *should be vocally fairly distinct from each other. In the first performance as part of* The Vanity Case *this was achieved by giving the* PROFESSOR *a tremendous, childlike enthusiasm and a slight central European accent.*

The PROFESSOR *and the* INTERVIEWER *sit one on each side of a table upon which the various exhibits will be able to be displayed clearly. Their clothes should reveal, though not too outrageously, that the sketch is set in the future. There is music which fades as the lights come up.*

INTERVIEWER: Good evening. Primitive societies of the past have always captured the imagination; none more so, perhaps, than that of the twentieth century. Historical novelists cannot resist that flamboyant twentieth century Gentleman of

the Road – the Sales Rep. A swashbuckling
figure in his Acrilan suit and his glittering
Cortina. In our dreams we travel with him to
outlandish destinations – Ongar, Dudley,
and the highly improbable Stoke-on-Trent.
We thrill to the very words 'Motorway
Services', rich in romance and high drama.
But what is the truth behind the fiction?
Tonight my guest is Professor George Edel-
mann – archaeologist, historian and writer.

EDELMANN: Good evening!

INTERVIEWER: Professor, just how many of our romantic
illusions about the twentieth century are you
going to let us keep?

EDELMANN: Well, we have recently been excavating a
number of very important sites in ————,
(*an appropriately local reference may be
inserted*) which were inhabited during the
early 1980s, and a very definite picture is
beginning to emerge.

INTERVIEWER: A picture of what?

EDELMANN: Of drabness, frustration, superficiality.

INTERVIEWER: Just what you had predicted, in fact?

EDELMANN: Exactly! We're very excited! For instance,
(*he brings from his bag a five-pound note in a
plastic case and holds it up*) I wonder if you
can guess what this is? Isn't that beautiful?

INTERVIEWER: (*Reverently*) It is. It's exquisite! May I? (*He
takes it very, very carefully, holding it up to
the light and examining it*) Very delicately
traced and coloured. It obviously meant a
great deal to whoever possessed it.

EDELMANN: Precisely. It was, in fact, a love-token!

INTERVIEWER: A love-token!

EDELMANN: Yes, indeed. People used to give these to
other people instead of love. Husbands, for
instance, would give a great many of these to
turf-accountants, publicans, second-hand
car salesmen and so on. And one or two to
their wives.

INTERVIEWER: Extraordinary! What else have you got there?

EDELMANN: Ah, well! Let's see what you make of this
one! (*He delves into his bag and brings out a
small, portable television set*)

INTERVIEWER: Goodness! Now this is a bit more sophisticated!

EDELMANN: Isn't it just!

INTERVIEWER: This looks like some sort of display screen ...

EDELMANN: Very good!

INTERVIEWER: And these knobs – could they be for adjustment?

EDELMANN: Very good indeed! Yes. You see, the twentieth century ... (*he searches for the right word*) civilisation – as we sometimes call it – was terrified of the open air: they didn't dare go out and do anything. Instead, they stayed inside and watched other people doing things on this box. It let them know what was going on.

INTERVIEWER: And it entertained them, presumably?

EDELMANN: (*Surprised*) We have no evidence of that, no.

INTERVIEWER: I see. Do we know why they were so frightened of the open air?

EDELMANN: (*Back on safe ground*) Well, there are a number of theories. One theory claims that there was no such thing as fresh air; another puts it down to a fear of the Little People.

INTERVIEWER: (*Indulgently*) Oh, come now, Professor! You don't mean that the twentieth century actually believed in fairies?

EDELMANN: Oh, they most certainly did! Yes! It was said that, during the hours of darkness while mortals were asleep, a band of fairy-folk known as The Vandals would skip mischievously about the town, painting things the wrong colour, smashing windows and tipping machinery into canals!

INTERVIEWER: (*Drily*) Presumably no one ever saw them!

EDELMANN: Ah! It was considered bad luck to come across one of these troupes at their sport. Apparently, if their merrymaking were interrupted, they would throw you to the ground, skipping merrily about you and playfully thrusting broken bottles into your face! (*He smiles at this charming conceit*)

INTERVIEWER: Well, Professor, you mentioned drabness and frustration earlier – let's move on to something more exciting: superficiality.

EDELMANN: Ah, well! This brings me straight away to religion. In almost every dwelling which we excavated we came across a similar icon, again and again. Now, when something turns up as often as this it is bound to be important and is usually of religious significance.

INTERVIEWER: And what is this icon?

EDELMANN: Two primitive figures, dressed in the costume of the day. One male, one female. These figures were also to be found on sundry drinking-vessels, clothes, and on tiny pieces of gummed paper with perforations. This is an almost perfect example. (*He brings out and stands up the famous engagement poster of Prince Charles and Lady Diana: she is wearing a blue dress and he stands behind her with one hand appearing over her shoulder. This is what* EDELMANN *points out first.*) That is the male on the ... er ... right, and the female on the left. You will notice the third arm, protruding from the neck (*He indicates it*); a symbol of fertility. And here, you see, (*Charles's ears*) the huge ears of the listening god.

INTERVIEWER: (*Much impressed*) It's wonderful, isn't it, to look at these and to think that they were actually used all those years ago?

EDELMANN: It is a thrill, isn't it?

INTERVIEWER: What else can you show us, Professor?

EDELMANN: (*Diving into his big bag again*) Well, this is quite interesting. (*He brings out a cheap spirits glass*) We've cleaned it up and ...

INTERVIEWER: Ah! Now I do recognise that: that's a ritual drinking vessel.

EDELMANN: Very good indeed! Yes! But of social rather than religious significance. When visitors came to a house, this would be filled with a libation of clear liquid known as gin (*he pronounces it with a hard g*) or jinn. Then a ritual of great richness and complexity would begin. The host would say a Word of Invocation 'Chuz' (*he performs the appropriate action*) and take a sip. One of the guests would then reply with the Acceptable Response 'Ah, That's Better' and then all those present would sit down in a small circle and insult those who were not there. This could take the form of extreme abuse, or be

simply lies and exaggerations. After this a
meal would be eaten.

INTERVIEWER: And this had a tradition too?

EDELMANN: Only one. It had to be more ornate and look
more expensive than the one the visitors had
previously provided for *them*.

INTERVIEWER: But there must have been times when they
could just relax and enjoy themselves.
Didn't they ever play games?

EDELMANN: Hmmmm. Well. It depends what you mean
by games. They were certainly great hoaxers!

INTERVIEWER: Hoaxers. Could you explain that?

EDELMANN: Well, there was one very very silly thing
which the whole country would join in with
every four or five years. It was called Polling
or Polling. (*He pronounces the second word
with a short o to rhyme with 'lolling'*)

INTERVIEWER: (*Taking this second pronunciation*) Polling?

EDELMANN: Yes. The derivation of the word is obvious
enough: to imitate the action of a parrot.
People would go into a kind of artificial
cupboard and place a cross on a small piece
of paper. Afterwards, the crosses would be
counted. And the pieces of paper ... thrown
away.

INTERVIEWER: (*Puzzled*) It had no effect on anything else?

EDELMANN: No, no, no. None whatsoever.

INTERVIEWER: Well, Professor, it has been a fascinating
discussion, but we have almost run out of
time. Is there any other small thing you can
show us before we finish?

EDELMANN: Yes, I've got ... (*rummages in bag*) ... er ...
ah! Now, you've done awfully well so far,
but I wonder if you can tell me what this is?
(*He produces a copy of the* TV TIMES)

INTERVIEWER: Well, now. It's obviously written by somebody called T.V. Times ...

EDELMANN: Good.

INTERVIEWER: Um ... A catalogue of some sort?

EDELMANN: Aaaaah, no! I can't let you have that, I'm
afraid. This is, in fact, a twentieth-century
Bible!

(*Blackout. Music*)

One in a Million
by Richard Everett

SIMON SLIME, *slick, fast and dominant with an American accent.*
BOBBY GOBSTOPPER, *a little boy. Can be played by anyone of any age or even sex.* SIR REGINALD MONEYBAGS, *a middle-aged and large man. Don't hesitate to go 'over the top' in dressing these three characters.* MR B. LEVER, *a very ordinary young man. Avoid making him smug!*

A TV studio. Almost any space will do. It's the people that will establish the atmosphere so use as many as possible, dress them in jeans and sweatshirts and let them rush about with headphones and clipboards at the beginning.
Think 'cartoon'. Make everything larger than life, so the sketch is bold and colourful. The bigger the better, the faster the funnier!

A typical TV quiz show is about to begin. Over the microphone we hear a drum roll followed by this announcement:

VOICE OFF: Ladies and gentlemen, Town TV proudly presents 'One in a Million'! – and here is your host for tonight … Si-iii-mon Slime! (*Canned applause, cheers etc., as compère leaps onto the stage with all the sickening charm and energy of the TV game-show host. He has a mid-Atlantic accent. Outrageous clothing.*)

SLIME: Hello, good evening and welcome to this week's fun-packed edition of 'One in a Million'. The show that gives three contestants the chance to become, once again, a normal human being! (*Applause, lots of cheers and encouraging the audience to join in*) Have you had a good week?!

CHORUS: (*off*) Ye-e-s thank you, Slimey!

SLIME: Good, well, let's move right along with the show. Our first contestant comes from Tottington near Manchester. He is a banker

and has been banking on almost everything
since he was twenty years of age! Ha! Ha!
But seriously, folks, he holidays in the south
of France, has a big house with thirty-nine
bedrooms, seventeen bathrooms and a
swimming pool. He drives six Mercedes Benz,
two Rolls Royces and a Range Rover – not
all at the same time, I hope! Ha! He employs
three chauffeurs, two cooks, four gardeners
and a pack of Alsatian guard dogs. Think
he's got everything he wants? … Not quite!
So successful has he been at handling other
people's money that he has in fact become …
a safety deposit box! He's here tonight to see
if he can win back his normal human identity.
Will you please welcome … Sir Reginald
Moneybags! (*Applause, music etc. A fat man
enters with a large box on his head with his
face showing through. The box is painted to
look like a safety deposit box, perhaps with a
large handle at the top. He also wears sun
glasses with pound signs painted on the glass*)

SLIME: Good evening, Reggie.

REGGIE: Good evening.

SLIME: Now ust to remind you and the viewers at
home o the rules once again. You have to
answer three questions correctly in order to
take home tonight's star prize … which is …
Horace? (HORACE's *silky voice is heard
speaking intimately over the microphone.
Lots of 'oohs' and 'aahs' off, as* HORACE
describes the star prize)

HORACE: (*Off*) Tonight's star prize, Simon, is a complete package comprising: a sense of humour
and a suite of six loyal friends to laugh at
your jokes, the courage to stand up for your
convictions; the ability to cry without feeling
ashamed of yourself; the capacity to care
about those less fortunate than yourself and
finally a magnificent and luxurious ready-to-
assemble kit containing conclusive evidence
that there is more to this brief life than meets
the eye. (*Applause, cheers, etc.*)

SLIME: O.K. Are you all set Reggie?

REGGIE: All set, yes.

SLIME: Bet you've got your eye on that 'sense of humour' haven't you?

REGGIE: Well I'd like the 'capacity to care about those less fortunate than myself' actually.

SLIME: Really? And why's that?

REGGIE: Well, the wife's watching at home and I think she would appreciate it.

SLIME: O.K. Here we go then. First question: when a baby is born, who or what does it most need? Is it (a) a cheque for a thousand pounds; (b) the Abbey habit; or (c) a mother? (*Pause*) Take your time now.

REGGIE: A ... mother?

SLIME: Is the right answer!!! (SLIME *encourages audience applause and cheers*).

SLIME: Second question. Here we go: which of the following does a starving child need most – is it (a) sympathy; (b) a letter of encourage-ment telling him that the recession is bound to blow over soon; or (c) food?

REGGIE: Um ...

SLIME: Think about it, Reggie.

REGGIE: I would say ... sympathy.

SLIME: I'm sorry, Reggie. Not the right answer – you can't survive on a sympathy sandwich. And I'll bet you knew it all the time. I'm so sorry ... a round of applause ladies and gentlemen, for our very good contestant who is *not* tonight's One in a Million. (*Applause, music etc*)
Our second contestant tonight is from the younger generation. He is aged ten and lives with his parents in Guildford. He has his very own sweet shop and his bedroom is wall-papered with liquorice allsorts.
He takes his own supply of sweet cigarettes to school every day and he is allowed to stay up as late as he likes, watching television and eating as many sherbert lemons as he can. Think he's got everything he wants ...? Not quite!!! He has become so greedy and selfish that, even at this young age, he has ... in fact ... turned into a boiled sweet. Will you please welcome ... Master Bobby Gobstop-per!!! (*Applause, music, cheers etc. Enter* BOY

in short trousers wrapped in cellophane and tied top and bottom. Perhaps a hat of some description)

SLIME: All set, Bobby?

BOBBY: I think so.

SLIME: You're not nervous are you?

BOBBY: A bit – yes.

S∟IME: Well there's nothing to be afraid of. What particular bit of the star prize have you got your eye on?

ьOBBY: I wouldn't mind a few loyal friends.

SLIME: A few loyal friends eh? Well, we'll see what we can do. Three questions Bobby, here's the first: you have a bag of sweets and you are with your classmates. Which of the following should you do – (a) hide the sweets down the front of your trousers; (b) lock yourself in the broom cupboard and gorge yourself silly; or (c) hand them round.

BOBBY: I ... er ...

SLIME: Take your time, Bobby.

BOBBY: I'd lock myself in the broom cupboard ... I think?

SLIME: You think?

BOBBY: Sometimes, yes. But when I'm not thinking I hand them round.

SLIME: Hand them round is the right answer! Boy, that was a close one! Had us on the edge of our seats there, Bobby! O.K. That's one out of three, so those 'loyal friends' are just around the corner, Bobby. Second question we're all with you, and here we go: it's your mother's birthday, Bobby. You have fifty pence in your pocket so should you (a) hide the money and tell mummy you're skint; (b) hide the money and tell daddy you're skint ... or (c) go without bubble gum that week and buy your mother a lovely bunch of flowers?

BOBBY: I think ... I should ...

SLIME: Yes, Bobby? Gotta hurry you, I'm afraid.

BOBBY: Tell 'em both I was skint!

SLIME: I'm sorry, Bobby. That was the wrong answer. Can anyone in our studio audience tell Bobby what he should have done?

(*Hopefully someone in the audience volunteers the right answer. If not – ad lib!*)

SLIME: A round of applause, ladies and gentlemen, for our brave contestant who leaves the show without friends and without being One in a Million! (*Applause, music, etc.*)

And so to our final contestant who lives in Sutton Coldfield, has a wife and three children and enjoys a simple but active life, caring for his neighbour and doing an honest day's work. Think he's got everything he wants ... ? Not quite!!! Because our next contestant is so convinced of the existence of God that he has in fact become a ... Chrrristian! He's here tonight because he, too, wants to win the 'One in a Million' star prize. Let's find out why and let's meet ... Mr B. Lever!! (*Applause, music etc. Enter a very ordinary looking man*) Welcome to the show Mr B. Lever.

B LEVER: Thank you.

SLIME: Can I call you BL?

B LEVER: So long as it doesn't stand for British Leyland, yes.

SLIME: Oh! that's really funny! BL ... British Leyland! ... I like that! (SLIME *suddenly whispers aggressively to* BL.) I'll do the jokes O.K.?! ... Well now BL and what particular part of the star prize have you got your eye on tonight?

B LEVER: All of it really.

SLIME: All of it! I would never have believed it of one who seems to have so much ... But then I'm not a believer am I?!! Ha! Ha! ... But enough of the chat, let's move right along with the questions. First question, BL: you have a problem, a personal problem that is bothering you. Which is the first thing you should do –

B LEVER: Pray about it.

SLIME: I beg your pardon?

B LEVER: Pray about it. I pray about it.

SLIME: But I haven't given you the alternatives yet!

B LEVER: There is no alternative. I wouldn't know what else to do.

SLIME: Well, BL, I have to tell you that … it *is* the right answer!! (*Applause, cheers etc.*) My word! Quick on the draw eh? O.K. Here we go with the second question: which of the following ingredients will keep a family happy and a marriage together – fur coats for the wife and expensive toys for the children; the television on as much as possible … watching me of course! Ha! Ha! I'm sorry, that was an unfair distraction … or finally, love and care for the individual members of your family. Which of those three BL?

B LEVER: Love and care for the …

SLIME: Is the right answer!!! (*Applause, cheers and bells or sirens go to herald the jackpot*)

SLIME: That's two in a row and the star prize is yours, BL. But you can of course go for the jackpot bonus of a ten year supply of patience and understanding. Will you go for that, BL?

B LEVER: Yes I will.

SLIME: O.K. Here we go then. Your third question: if tonight's star prize was yours – which it already is – would you (a) throw it back in my face (b) take it home and never use it or (c) give it away.

B LEVER: I'd give it away without doubt.

SLIME: Being a believer I'm sure you would … and that is the right answer, ladies and gentlemen!!! My, what an evening this has turned out to be. Congratulations, BL and just tell me, because I'm sure that the viewers at home are dying to hear, why would you give it away?

B LEVER: Because when you've got it, you keep t by giving it away again.

SLIME: Wooh! Got a real head-case here oiks' Ha' So, who are you going to give all tne wonderful goodies in tonight's star prize to, BL? Anyone we know?

B LEVER: Oh yes.

SLIME: Someone in need no doubt

B LEVER: Could be

SLIME: Who?

B LEVER: You.

SLIME: Me?

B LEVER: Yes.

SLIME: Me!?!

B LEVER: If you want them.

SLIME: Want them?! ME!? Ha! Ha! What a joker this man is! What would I do with a sense of humour, BL?!

B LEVER: Heaven knows.

SLIME: And friends! Why would *I* need *friends*?!

B LEVER: I really couldn't say.

SLIME: And evidence that there's more to this brief life than meets the eye! Ha! What would I do with that?!!

B LEVER: Anything you like. I don't wish to seem unkind but I don't believe that you have a care in the world for anyone but yourself. You are quite friendless, and I have a shrewd suspicion that you live entirely for this awful and extremely *un*funny show. So, tonight, Simon Slime, no questions and no catches, a free gift and your chance to be … One in a Million! (*Embarrassed silence as* SLIME's *plastic smile slips for a second or two and then he collects himself again*)

SLIME: Ha! Ha! Well that's all we have time for tonight. So don't forget – next week … same time … Sii-imon Slime!! (*Music, applause etc.*) Bye everyone. Bye! (*Everyone exits as music and applause fades*)

Jonah's Journey
by Nigel Forde

NARRATOR ONE   NARRATOR TWO   JONAH   GOD   BOATMAN

There is not a great deal of intellectualising to do about this sketch. It stands or falls by the amount of colour, energy and commitment that is put into it.

When it was first produced, the two narrators became the whale when it appeared, draping themselves with a black curtain and squirting a water-pistol into the air. If, however, there are some keen types around who would like to spend a weekend with rolls of canvas, cardboard and hosepipes – well then, the whale is your oyster, to coin a phrase. If the whale is not played by the narrators, he should himself speak the two asterisked lines.

Theatre is a rich, painstaking and sophisticated art. But you can forget all that for this sketch; coarseness is the key!

GOD is a perpetual observer throughout the whole sketch and he must be seen to be controlling all the events. He should be seated somewhere, comfortably, and on high. The two NARRATORS stand, one on each side of the stage. JONAH is asleep in bed. Near him is a telephone.

NARRATOR ONE: Once upon a time there was a man called Jonah,
NARRATOR TWO: A bit of an individual, a bit of a loner.
NARRATOR ONE: A good sort of fellow
NARRATOR TWO: With a heart of gold,
NARRATOR ONE: But rather slow at doing what he was told.
(*The telephone bell rings. JONAH turns over and over in bed, pulling the clothes over his head and refusing to answer. The ringing gets fainter and fainter. This surprises JONAH. He sits up and looks to see why. He puts his ear very close to the phone whereupon it rings suddenly extremely loudly. He answers it.*)
JONAH: Hello? Gilgal 70663?
GOD: Is that Jonah?

JONAH: Yes. Jonah speaking.

GOD: God here.

JONAH: God who?

GOD: What do you mean, 'God who?'?

JONAH: Oh … Oh, sorry! Yes, yes … God. Quite! Good God – I mean … yes. What?

GOD: All right, Jonah. Now, calm down and listen slowly.

JONAH: Right.

GOD: I want you to pop across to Nineveh for me, if you wouldn't mind. They get a bit over-excited sometimes, and I thought you'd be just the chap to go and tell them to watch it or else. That sort of thing.

JONAH: Nineveh?

GOD: Nineveh.

JONAH: *Nineveh*??

GOD: Yes, Jonah, Nineveh: N for Nazareth, I for Israel, N for Nazareth, E for …

JONAH: But … Nineveh! I mean, do you realise how far it is to Nineveh? Do you … well, I suppose, being God, you *would* realise how far it is to Nineveh. To the nearest inch. But I mean … it's a bit short notice! I mean, it's too late now to book a Saver – I've … I've got to get packed, you see. There's my suitcase … there's …
(JONAH's *suitcase, all packed and labelled, whizzes on at God's behest*)
There's my suitcase … but then, ah! You see I need to be at home to keep away the rhinoceroses!

GOD: Jonah, there aren't any rhinoceroses around here.

JONAH: No. Well. You see how efficient I am?

GOD: Any other problems, Jonah?

JONAH: Er … well, I was thinking of going on my holidays pretty soon.

GOD: Anywhere special in mind, Jonah?

JONAH: I thought Wales might be nice …

GOD: Jonah!
(JONAH *puts down the phone, picks up his bag and goes*)

ONE: So he put on his coat and he put on his topper,

TWO: Picked up his passport and went off to Joppa.

ONE: Joppa?

TWO: Joppa.

ONE: He told God a whopper?

TWO: He took a boat for Tarshish, and now it doesn't rhyme.

(JONAH *arrives at the harbour. A* BOATMAN *is sitting in his boat. He is a Long John Silver type*)

JONAH: Ho there! Boatman!

BOATMAN: Haha! Ha! Haaaarrrggghh. Haharrrrrrrr. Belay there me hearties! Harrr!! Yezzurrrr??

JONAH: Where are you bound?

BOATMAN: Where am Oi bound? Haharrrrrrr! Ha ha ha harrrrrgggghhhh. Harrrgggghhhh!! (*Then, in perfect standard English*) Sorry, what was the question again?

JONAH: Where.Is.This.Ship.Going?

BOATMAN: 'Taint goin' nowhere, zur. 'Tis tied up! BUT … she'll be goin' to Tarshish, sir, shortly. And that ain't easy ter say! Step aboard, sir! Avast behind!

JONAH: Ooooh!

(JONAH *gets on to the boat and soon begins to hang over the side and look green*)

ONE: So Jonah went aboard and the ship set sail,

TWO: And very shortly after, it began to blow a gale.

ONE: The dark clouds gathered and the waves rose high,

TWO: The lightning flashed and thunder crashed along the purple sky.

ONE: The steep seas piled like a green rock-face,

TWO: And Jonah took his teeth out – just in case.

ONE: The boat was tossed and battered,

TWO: Doing forward rolls and flips,

ONE: And there weren't too many takers for the sausage, egg and chips.

BOATMAN: 'Scuse me, sir, but there's something I've been meaning to bring up.

JONAH: Yes, I know the feeling!

BOATMAN: Why aren't you prayin' loike the rest o' the lads?

JONAH: I can't pray! I'm running away from God!

GOD: (*Rather amused at the idea*) Running away from God!!

JONAH: You said that without moving your lips!

BOATMAN: Are you a nautical man, sir?

JONAH: Very nautical, yes. But I mean well.

BOATMAN: Then you'll understand that we have to lighten the load o' the ship?

JONAH: Oh, yes. Bags first!

BOATMAN: That's very obliging of you, sir.
(*He tips* JONAH *into the sea*)

JONAH: No, no, no! *The* bags first! Not *I* bags first!

BOATMAN: Sorry sir, I can't hear you above this terrible wind!

JONAH: What? I can't hear you above this terrible wind!
(*The boat disappears and* JONAH *is left swimming and miserable*)

ONE: Water, water everywhere, nor any drop to drink;

TWO: He was cold and he was lonely and his socks began to shrink.

ONE: The night drew in, the boat was gone, he thought it was the end,

TWO: But God knew what was going on and sent along a friend.
(GOD *signals and the whale appears, bearing down on* JONAH)

JONAH: Argghhhhh! Oooooh! Eeeeek! Oh no! A whale!!!

* ONE: (*Severely patient*) It's all right, it's all right! I'm not going to eat you!

GOD: Wrong!!

* ONE: Oh, sorry. In you come then!

JONAH: Oh no! Oh no! You won't get me in there! Not likely! There is no wayheyyyyyyyyy!!!!
(*He is swallowed by the whale*)

TWO: And wipe your feet first!

ONE: Make yourself comfortable!

TWO: There's some plankton in the cupboard.
(JONAH *makes a moaning protesting kind of howl*)

ONE: Hey, and no wailing! (*To* TWO) I say, d'you hear what I said? No *wail*ing! Hur hur!

TWO: That's right. Don't *blubber*! Eh? Eh?

ONE: Oh, *blubber*! Yeah! 'S good, that. Yeah!
(*During all this, the whale has progressed a little. As it comes round again the*

NARRATORS *stop it and call down to* JONAH)

ONE: Hey, Jonah!

JONAH: (*Sulkily*) What?

TWO: I bet you can't guess where you're going now.

JONAH: God knows *what's* happening.

ONE: Well done Jonah!

TWO: Good thinking, my mate!

ONE: You've got there at last!

JONAH: Eh? Got where?

ONE: Nineveh, actually.

JONAH: Nineveh?

TWO: Yes, Nineveh.

ONE: Nineveh: N for Naboth's vineyard, I for Idumea, N for Naboth's ...

JONAH: Oh, Nineveh!

TWO: That's right!

ONE: All change!

TWO: Mind the jaws!

ONE: Anyway –

TWO: Jonah got to Nineveh and did a lot of good.

ONE: He preached, and people started doing what they ought to should.
(JONAH *drops open a scroll à la newspaper vendor. It says in huge capitals 'SIN BAN BID SHOCK'*)

TWO: (*Pointing out the headline*) 'SIN BAN BID SHOCK' all the papers said.

ONE: (*As* JONAH *drops open second scroll with these words on it*) 'JONAH PREACHES WORD OF GOD'

JONAH: Nobody feared dead!

ONE: So Jonah learned the hard way what he always should have guessed –

TWO: The one thing worth remembering:

ONE:
TWO: } God always knows what's best.
JONAH:

The Interrogation
by Andrew Goreing

FIRST SECURITY OFFICER   SECOND SECURITY OFFICER
CENTURION

To be effective this must be performed with considerable speed and élan, so that the continual repetitions take on a rhythmic life of their own. Note that the actual dramatic form – the interrogation – has nothing to do with the content – the miracle – which is merely reported, not dramatised. This oblique approach to a story can sometimes bring out aspects that would remain obscure in a straightforward dramatisation. It also avoids competing directly with the original; a straightforward dramatisation can often simply inflate and make flabby a Bible passage which in its original form is vigorous, concise and dramatic.

This piece requires no more than the absolute minimum of props: a chair, a wallet with I.D. card, a cigarette lighter.

The two SECURITY OFFICERS *leap on the* CENTURION *and seize him by the arms.*

<blockquote>

CENT: Hey!?

FIRST S.O.: You're under arrest.

CENT: What? Me!?

SECOND S.O.: Yes, you.

CENT: But I'm a centurion!

FIRST S.O.: Are you going to come quietly?

CENT: (*Whispering*) But I'm a centurion. (*He is dragged backwards and plonked on a chair*)

FIRST S.O.: (*Flashing his I.D. card*) Occupying forces, Palestine, Internal Security, Military Branch.

CENT: What's going on?

FIRST S.O.: Do you admit it?

CENT: What?

FIRST S.O.: Do you admit it?

CENT: Admit what?

FIRST S.O.: Do you admit it???

</blockquote>

CENT: No.

FIRST S.O.: He denies it.

SECOND S.O.: Give him the third degree. (*A cigarette lighter is flashed in the* CENTURION*'s face*)

FIRST S.O.: Ah-ha!

CENT: No!

SECOND S.O.: Ah-ha!

FIRST S.O.: Confess!

CENT: I'm telling you nothing but my name, rank and number.

FIRST S.O.: Where were you on the afternoon of the fourteenth?

CENT: I don't have to say anything.

FIRST S.O.: Where were you on the afternoon of the fourteenth?

CENT: Marcus Placidus, Centurion, three-double-one-seven-six.

FIRST S.O.: What's your name, rank and number?

CENT: I was at home all day.

FIRST S.O.: Ah-ha!

SECOND S.O.: He admits it!

CENT: I admit nothing!

FIRST S.O.: He admits nothing.

SECOND S.O.: What does he deny?

FIRST S.O.: What do you deny?

CENT: I deny nothing!

FIRST S.O.: He denies nothing as well.

SECOND S.O.: He must deny *some*thing.

FIRST S.O.: Deny something!

CENT: I didn't do it!

FIRST S.O.: You didn't do it?

CENT: No!

FIRST S.O.: Do you admit nothing?

CENT: Yes.

SECOND S.O.: Do you deny nothing?

CENT: Yes.

FIRST S.O.: Do you deny that you admit nothing?

CENT: No.

SECOND S.O.: Are you Marcus Placidus?

CENT: Yes.

FIRST S.O.: Centurion?

CENT: Yes.

SECOND S.O.: Three-double-one-seven-six?

CENT: Yes.

FIRST S.O.: Were you at home all day on the fourteenth?

CENT: Yes.

SECOND S.O.: Do you love the Jewish nation?

CENT: Yes.

FIRST S.O.: Did you build them a synagogue right here in Capernaum?

CENT: Yes.

FIRST S.O.: Ah-ha!

CENT: Yes.

FIRST S.O.: And now – !

CENT: Yes.

FIRST S.O.: This is the final straw!

CENT: Yes.

FIRST S.O.: That on the aforesaid fourteenth you did fraternise with a certain Jew, to wit, a preacher and travelling quack!

CENT: No.

FIRST S.O.: No?

SECOND S.O.: A very serious charge, conspiring with the native population –

CENT: I didn't.

FIRST S.O.: Why did you meet this travelling quack?

CENT: I didn't.

FIRST S.O.: All right, why didn't you meet this travelling quack?

CENT: My servant was ill.

FIRST S.O.: Ah-ha! What was wrong with your servant?

CENT: Measles.

FIRST S.O.: The fatal kind.

FIRST & SECOND: EEurgh!

CENT: Precisely.

FIRST S.O.: And you wanted him cured?

CENT: Yes.

SECOND S.O.: So you did meet this travelling quack?

CENT: I did not.

FIRST S.O.: You rang him up?

CENT: No.

SECOND S.O.: You sent him a postcard?

CENT: No.

FIRST S.O.: No?

CENT: I sent the Jewish elders to him with a message.

FIRST S.O.: Ah-ha!

SECOND S.O.: Saying what?

CENT: I said

FIRST S.O.: You said

CENT: I am a man accustomed to authority.

FIRST S.O.: Authority.

CENT: I say 'Do that.' (*Pointing*)

FIRST S.O.: Do what?

CENT: Do that.

FIRST S.O.: (*Looking around for it*) Where?

CENT: And it is done.

FIRST S.O.: It is?

CENT: Therefore, Lord, do not come under my roof.

FIRST S.O.: Your roof.

CENT: For I am not worthy. Just say the word and my servant shall be healed.

FIRST S.O.: You said.

CENT: I said.

FIRST S.O.: Is that it?

CENT: That's it.

SECOND S.O.: And is your servant healed?

CENT: Perfectly well, thank you.

FIRST S.O.: So this man did cure your servant?

CENT: Yes.

SECOND S.O.: Come on, did he or didn't he?

CENT: He did.

FIRST S.O.: Answer the question!

CENT: He did heal him!

SECOND S.O.: Do you deny that your servant is healed?

CENT: No.

FIRST S.O.: Do you admit it?

CENT: I do.

FIRST S.O.: So! You admit that this man miraculously healed your servant of a fatal disease without even entering the house!

CENT: I do.

FIRST S.O.: (*Fractional pause*) What!???

(*Blackout*)

Service with a Smile
by Nigel Forde

One CANTOR, *possibly robed: the other singers are members of the congregation and should be dressed as differently as possible from each other. Lots of hats! The whole of the sketch is sung.*

The actor playing the CANTOR *intones the words 'Our Father' on a G. The rest of the cast join in with 'which art in heaven' and the whole prayer continues on a unison G. The pauses/breaths are marked by commas. The 'Oh crumbs' ('Amen') is the usual perfect cadence after a collect. The chord can be constructed in a number of different ways, but the most straightforward is:*

Our Father ...

The psalm itself should be sung to a fairly bright chant as the Venite itself would be. Any tune designated for the Venite or the beginning of the Te Deum in the psalter should do. The original tune used by RLTC in The Vanity Case *was No. 84 in* The New Cathedral Psalter Chants: *J. Corfe from H. Lawes. It is impossible here to explain the system of pointing psalms in the Anglican Service, and styles differ. If the cast is unused to singing psalms, the best thing to do would be to find a record of a well-known Cathedral choir singing psalms and emulate their method.*

CANTOR: Let us pray. Our Father –
    ALL: Which art in heaven and therefore can be
          ignored most of the time, hallowed be thy
          name, except when things really get on top
          of me.
          Thy kingdom come, but not just yet, thank
          you,
          Thy will be done, on earth as it is in heaven,
          as long as it doesn't make things too difficult
          for us.

Give us this day our daily bread, oh *yes*!
And forgive us our trespasses, oh *yes*! As we
may or may not forgive them that trespass
against us, because they do it time after time
and really, if you knew what it was like, well,
you'd think twice about forgiving them too,
so you'll understand. Won't you? Please?
And lead us not into temptation when there's
anyone else there to tell on us;
but deliver us from evil or it'll be your fault
anyway.
For thine is the kingdom, the power and the
glory, for ever and ever,
Oh crumbs. (ALL *stand. A new chord is given
if necessary.*)

*O come, let us sing unto the Lord: let us
heartily rejoice in the strength of our salvation.*
*Let us come before his presence with
thanksgiving: and shew ourselves glad in him
with psalms.*
*I'll go along with that: especially on such a
glorious day.*
*Good morning Mrs Marchant, Colonel
Fanshaw, Mr Keyte, Mr and Mrs Barker:
and all the little Barkers.*
*For the Lord is a great God: and a great King
above all gods.*
*In his hands are all the corners of the earth:
and the strength of the hills is his also.*
*What a poetic image: but things aren't quite as
simple as a lot of the church would have us
think.*
*How can you turn a blind eye: to what is
going on in South America, the unemployment figures, the rising crime-rate. cot-deaths,
cancer, the threat of nuclear war tne third
world, and the terrible price of lobsters.*
*The sea is his and he made it: and his hands
prepared the dry land.*
*O come, let us worship and fall down: and
kneel before the Lord our Maker.*
*This is really absurd: do they mean us to take
it seriously?*
Why is the Bible so simplistic? After all

we're not children any more,
I'm nearly forty years old.
Forty years long was I grieved with this
generation and said: It is a people that do err
in their hearts, for they have not known my
ways.
Unto whom I sware in my wrath: that they
should not enter into my rest.

Glory be to the ———, and to the ———:
and to the ——— ———.
Fill in the blanks as seems appropriate: to
make a well known phrase or saying.

Lexicon
by Nigel Forde

DAPHNE ROGET, *the bank manager* MAN WOMAN TOMMY
MR PETTY WRITER

The content of this sketch represents something very close to my heart both as a Christian and as a writer: the preservation of the richness and the accuracy of our language. Once language becomes corrupted and inaccurate, then thought becomes so too; and so do ideas themselves. We end up not only with no means of thinking clearly, but with very little to think about. All too often language is used not to express something clearly and unambiguously, but to cloak ignorance, to make a fine noise without the added burden of meaning, to disguise deceit. Those are intentional corruptions. Even more insidious are those due to laziness, fashion and even vanity. Theology is founded on grammar – listen to any first-class Bible teacher. What if those foundations crumble?

The satire in LEXICON is aimed at all sorts and conditions of men. It may seem that the meat of the sketch is to be found in the second half, but this in itself depends very much on the atmosphere engendered by the opening and the various eccentrics who come to the bank for assistance. In small companies doublings can be made as long as it remains clear that every character is different and that none returns.

The BANK MANAGER *is not involved in the first part of the action but should be seated at his desk involved in some innocuous activity such as doing* The Times *crossword or checking his stock of subordinate adverbial clauses.* DAPHNE, *the cashier, is at another desk with a telephone and some files. It is to her counter that the customers come. Only* DAPHNE *and the* MANAGER *are onstage when the lights come up.* DAPHNE's *telephone rings. She lifts the receiver.*

DAPHNE: Good morning, sir. Yes, this is the Word Bank ... Just a moment, sir, and I'll check your account. (*She opens a ledger*) Well, sir, according to our books, your current vocabulary does seem to be rather overdrawn at the moment … Yes … Mainly adverbs. Do you have a latent vocabulary? No. Well, you can, of course, give the impression of a very extensive vocabulary by the use of one of our Word Conversion Units. Oh, yes, sir, very easily! You simply add the word 'wise' on to any noun or present participle: education-wise, viewingwise, creativitywise … Not at all, sir; it costs nothing – just remember to avoid all intelligent conversation. (*Laughing*) No, no, sir; not intellectual – *intelligent*! Thank you, sir. Goodbye! (*She turns to the first customer who has just entered*) Now sir?

MAN: I wonder if you can help me? Do you change words here?

DAPHNE: Meaning or spelling, sir?

MAN: (*Who hadn't expected things to be so complicated*) Er … meaning, really, I suppose. I've got this word 'dull'; I've used it quite a lot and it's getting a bit – well, dull, really …

DAPHNE: (*Brightly*) Yes, we can change that for you sir. How would you like it? Colourless, achromatic, hueless, pale, pallid, muddy, weak, faint, heavy, leaden, dun? Or would you prefer wan, sallow, dingy, ashen, ghastly, discoloured, lacklustre?

MAN: Well, I was thinking more of – you know .. dull …

DAPHNE: How about unexciting, flat, weary, stale, unprofitable, inert, stolid, dim?

MAN: Ah! That would do marvellously. Yes! Thank you. Goodbye.

DAPHNE: Thank you, sir. (*To next customer who enters as man leaves*) Good morning.

WOMAN: Good morning. I'd like to open an account here if I may.

DAPHNE: Of course, madam. Have you ever had an account anywhere else?

WOMAN: Oh no! No, no, no. I've always used second-hand words and ideas; old ones I learned from my parents.

DAPHNE: I'm afraid I'll have to ask you your occupation.

WOMAN: Arts critic.

DAPHNE: (*Rather impressed*) Arts critic! Then may I offer you a free gift, just to start off your account?

WOMAN: Oh, how kind! What is it?

DAPHNE: It's a basic kit, just to cover your first dozen or so reviews. Some people (*confidentially*) make them last a lot longer, of course; and we do have one or two very eminent critics on our books who have been using this basic kit for their entire careers!

WOMAN: It doesn't look very big.

DAPHNE: (*Slightly affronted*) I think you'll find it's adequate, madam. Look – half a dozen 'interesting', half a dozen 'mature', a *dozen* 'significant'. Four each of 'provincial', 'neo-classic', 'introspective' and 'luminous'; useful phrases such as 'essential dichotomy', 'intellectual climate', 'fundamental principles underlying'; some German and French expressions and (*proudly, conspiratorially*) one or two rather *long* words!

WOMAN: Thank you very much! (WOMAN *exits*)

DAPHNE: Not at all! Next please. (TOMMY *enters.* TOMMY *is a typical, seedy, but immensely good-natured variety comedian: loud check jacket, revolving bow-tie, bowler, cigar, buttonhole. He is very pleased with life*)

TOMMY: Heheyyyy! Usual, please luv!!

DAPHNE: (*Delighted to see him*) Hallo, Tommy! How did the Palladium go?

TOMMY: He, he!! Great! It were *great*!

DAPHNE: Here we are, then. Mothers-in-law, honeymoon hotels, bras, bottoms and knicker-elastic.

TOMMY: He, he! Thanks, luv! (TOMMY *goes, chuckling, and* MR PETTY *enters. He is a boring little man, cycle-clips, grey gabardine, huge gauntlets and a crash-helmet*)

DAPHNE: Yes, sir?

PETTY: Wolled you haive swich a thong as a pimplet I could rode?

DAPHNE: (*Totally baffled but polite*) A what, sir?

PETTY: (*Distinctly*) A pimplet.

DAPHNE: A … pimplet … ?

PETTY: (*Thinking he may have the wrong term*) Pimplet … er … pamfrit … pomplefrit?

DAPHNE: (*Guessing*) Pamphlet?

PETTY: Ahhh! Pamphlet! Pamphlet. (*He tries again*)

Wolled you haive swich a thong as a *pam-phlet* I could rode?

DAPHNE: A pamphlet about what?

PETTY: My dour liddy, a pamphlet about pronoun-calotion!

DAPHNE: Pronunciation?

PETTY: (*Pleased*) You've hot the nile on the heed! (*In confidence*) I finned grote dafticully in spoking preepuley.

DAPHNE: (*Producing a booklet*) Well, sir, you could try that one.

PETTY: (*Leafs through it*) Hmmmmmm. Yes. This seems a very helpful little booklet indeed. Simple without being patronising and very, very clear. (*He hands it towards her*) Thinks for the opportannity to glonk atty ... (*He withdraws it again*) ... er ... I *think* I'll take it with me. (*He goes. The* WRITER, *who has just entered, watches him go with some amusement*)

DAPHNE: We do get some funny types in here. Still, live and let live, each to his own, variety is the spice of life! Er ... *was* it platitudes you wanted, sir?

WRITER: No, not really. Not at all, in fact. I'm writing a book and some poems about our attitudes to living and how they correspond, or other-wise, to truth; what moral purpose there is to life, and why we seem to fall short of attain-ing it.

DAPHNE: (*Slightly unsure*) Is this for *Punch*, sir?

WRITER: No, no; it's a serious work. I've approached these questions before, perhaps skirted round them. Now I want to tackle them in more depth.

DAPHNE: (*Ex cathedra*) 'Meaningful'.

WRITER: (*Slightly baffled*) Sorry?

DAPHNE. It's a word you'll need: 'meaningful'.

WRITER: (*Kindly but firmly*) Er ... no, I don't think so.

DAPHNE. Oh, yes. Take my word for it. 'Meaningful' and 'aspirations'. Both very fashionable.

WRITER: Yes. I'm not particularly keen on finding the fashionable word. I want the right one.

DAPHNE: Same thing, sir!

WRITER: What is?

DAPHNE: 'Right' and 'fashionable'.

WRITER: Oh, I don't think so – necessarily.

DAPHNE: (*Patronisingly but not unkindly*) Look, sir – I have hundreds of people in here every day asking for words and phrases. I know the sort of terms that are being bandied about these days: the sort people want to hear, and I can tell you ...

WRITER: I'm sure you're absolutely right, but that's not what I'm concerned with. I'm looking for the truth.

DAPHNE: (*Warning him*) Ah, ah! You can't use that word, sir!

WRITER: What word?

DAPHNE: 'Truth': it's not legal tender any more. I suppose you could use it if you wanted to talk about *a* truth, but not *the* truth.

WRITER: Look, do you think I could see the manager?

DAPHNE: Yes, sir – I think you'd better! (*Turns to* MANAGER'S *desk and calls*) Mr Roget! (WRITER *walks through to* ROGET'S *desk.* ROGET *rises, smiling. He is suave, helpful, and won't give an inch*)

ROGET: Ah, greetings, salutations, welcome, good-day, hello!

WRITER: Er ... hello. I'm having a bit of difficulty ...

ROGET: Ah, difficulty, hardship, trial, tribulation, vicissitude of ...

WRITER: (*Cutting him off as politely as possible*) Yes. Exactly. My particular ... (*He gestures vaguely in order to avoid saying 'difficulty' again and setting* ROGET *off on another hunt-the-synonym.* ROGET *nods agreement*) is in obtaining the words I need for a new book I'm writing. (ROGET *perks up at this*) I wonder if you could help me?

ROGET: (*Expansively*) Sit down, dear sir, read me your list and I will endeavour to assist you.

WRITER: Right. Thank you. (*Shoots a quick triumphant glance at* DAPHNE, *but she is busy*) 'Understanding'.

ROGET: Yes.

WRITER: 'Discussion'.

ROGET: Fine.

WRITER: 'Elementary', 'divulge', 'grasshopper'.

'ei ;eways'.

ROGET: No trouble there.

WRITER: 'Byzantine', 'cursory', 'folded', 'Old Trafford' ...

ROGET: (*Very Lady Bracknell*) 'Old Trafford'??

WRITER: For a sporting metaphor.

ROGET: Ah! The elegant trope! Yes, yes, yes, yes!

WRITER: Yes. (*Back to his list*) 'Perfect'.

ROGET: (*Matter-of-fact*) No.

WRITER: (*Shocked*) What?

ROGET: (*With exactly the same inflection as before*) No.

WRITER: 'Perfect'??

ROGET: (*Firmly and conclusively*) No! Sorry, sir. Inflation, you see? 'Perfect' doesn't mean anything any more.

WRITER: But this is ridiculous!

ROGET: (*Calmly*) Not at all ridiculous, sir. I can let you have five 'very's' and a 'good'; even an 'extremely' and a 'good', but not a 'perfect'.

WRITER: Look, I'll admit that nothing in this life can actually be perfect ...

ROGET: Then why debase the language, sir?

WRITER: Because I'm talking about ideals.

ROGET: (*Shakes his head*) Not on, sir, I'm afraid. Ideals aren't worth the paper they're printed on. Haven't been legal tender since ... ooooh, since the war.

WRITER: All right, all right. (*Tries a different tack*) 'Absolute'?

ROGET: Nope. Same thing applies, I'm afraid. There *are* no absolutes. (*Chuckles in a fatherly sort of way*) I don't know! You author chappies are all the same! Wanting to push language as far as it can go; not an ounce of concern as to whether the concept is relevant to the man-in-the-street. The public won't stand for this sort of thing!

WRITER: What about 'beauty'?

ROGET: (*Checking*) Daphne?

DAPHNE: Sorry, Mr Roget, we're right out!

ROGET: Ah ...

WRITER: Why?

ROGET: There's no call for it any more, sir. (*Tries him with an alternative*) 'Functionality' ... ?

WRITER: (*Takes no notice*) What about 'love'?

ROGET: (*Thinks for a moment*) 'Sex'?

WRITER: No; 'love'.

ROGET: (*Eagerly*) Another sporting term?

WRITER: No!

ROGET: No ... (*He was afraid it wasn't*) Well, so long as you don't use it *too* specifically, I suppose we *could* let you have 'love', yes.

WRITER: Well, that's *something*! 'Truth'?

DAPHNE: Ah, ah! I've told you about that. (*To* ROGET) I've told him about that.

ROGET: Never mind, sir; we can do better than 'truth' can't we? How about 'reality'?

WRITER: It's not the same thing.

ROGET: (*Firmly*) I'm sorry, sir, but I have it down here, quite clearly, in my list of current synonyms – 'truth' equals 'reality'.

WRITER: Well, if truth equals reality why can't I use truth instead of reality?

ROGET: Don't make it any more, sir. They only make reality these days.

WRITER: (*With sudden inspiration*) Got it! I've got it! You must have these!

ROGET: (*Excited at this new challenge*) Try me, sir!

WRITER: 'Good' and 'bad'!

ROGET: (*Tiny pause. Then playfully*) I've got just the word for you sir!

WRITER: (*Excited*) Yes?

ROGET: Yes! (*Contemptuously*) Naïve.

WRITER: But ... surely ... 'good' and 'bad' – they're so basic!

ROGET: 'Good' equals 'I like'; 'bad' equals 'I do not like'.

WRITER: No, it doesn't!! Look! I want a dozen 'truths', a dozen 'rights' a dozen 'wrongs', half a case of 'morals', half a case of 'immorals' and a large packet of ...

ROGET: Sir! (*Patiently*) I am running a twentieth-century word-store. I can't let you have any of those words! I couldn't give you a guarantee with any single one of them! And you'd never find a market for that kind of vocabulary: the public doesn't understand what half those words mean!

WRITER: Ah! So they do mean *something*!!

ROGET: Sir. Just because you don't understand the meaning of a word doesn't mean that the word has a meaning.

WRITER: Pardon?

ROGET: 'Gosbritt'.

WRITER: What?

ROGET: 'Gosbritt'.

WRITER: What does that mean?

ROGET: Precisely! It means absolutely nothing! No, I suggest you stick to solid, objective words like 'billiards' and 'upholstery'. You'll have no problems with those.

WRITER: No problems! (*He gets up and strides about. ROGET remains suave*) That's it, isn't it? No problems: that's the whole of your philosophy. Whatever we do we mustn't force ourselves to think. Oh, no!

ROGET: Sir …

WRITER: That's the last thing we want. Let's treat life like a pre-packed TV dinner: take out all the nasty bits in case they happen to be nutritious.

ROGET: If you'd listen to me …

WRITER: No! You listen to me for a moment. (*Whips out a slim volume*) I've got an advanced English Grammar in my hand – and it's *loaded*! (*ROGET and DAPHNE are in a fair state of panic*) I want five thousand words in used syllables, or … or I'll anagrammatise this whole store! (*DAPHNE hastens to give him a pile of files*)

ROGET: (*Desperately*) No, no, no, no, no! Those verbs are unconjugated!

WRITER: (*Turning on him savagely*) Shut your prefix!

ROGET: (*Striving for calmness*) You won't get away with this, you know. You can be put into brackets for this sort of thing.

WRITER: Don't move. Or I'll split your infinitives!

(*Blackout*)

Final Resolution
by Richard Everett

MRS NITTER   MRS NATTER

A corner grocery stores. Can be as simple or as detailed as you like. The more detail the better so long as you have time to set up. For MRS NITTER *and* MRS NATTER, *opposites are best, e.g. one short and fat, one tall and thin; one smartly dressed, one a real mess; one with a magnificent hairdo, one in curlers, etc. Tentative suggestion – they could be played by two blokes, à la Les Dawson!*

MRS NATTER *enters a grocer's shop.* MRS NITTER *serves behind the counter.*

NATTER: Morning, Mrs Nitter.

NITTER: Morning, Mrs Natter.

NATTER: Happy New Year to you.

NITTER: And to you, Mrs Natter. What can I do for you?

NATTER: I'd like a large white cut loaf please.

NITTER: A large white cut loaf.

NATTER: A packet of frozen peas.

NITTER: Packet of frozen peas.

NATTER: And half a pound of New Year's resolutions.

NITTER: And half a pound of New Year's resolutions. Any particular brand?

NATTER: Well, what do you recommend?

NITTER: It all depends on what you want, really. We've got the standard package of resolutions which most people buy, but they don't keep.

NATTER: Can't you freeze them?

NITTER: Well, you can, but they have a nasty habit of going off after a few days. I can't think why they're so popular.

NATTER: Well, I do want something that's going to last, but at the same time there's no point in cluttering the place up with things I'm never going to use. Know what I mean?

NITTER: Oh, I do.

NATTER: I mean, it's only once a year, isn't it?

NITTER: It is.

NATTER: And resolutions are a bit like fireworks really ...

NITTER: They are.

NATTER: One big colourful flash and it's all forgotten. Know what I mean?

NITTER: Oh, I do. Well, what sort of New Year's resolutions are you looking for, then?

NATTER: Have you got anything in the 'start talking to the people next door' line?

NITTER: I'm afraid not, no.

NATTER: How about a 'give up a morning a week for charity'?

NITTER: I'm right out of those, I'm afraid.

NATTER: Oh. A 'talk less, listen more'?

NITTER: All gone.

NATTER: A 'stop hurling abuse at traffic wardens'?

NITTER: Nope.

NATTER: A 'stop queue-jumping at the post office'?

NITTER: Nope.

NATTER: A 'stop kicking the neighbour's cat', then?

NITTER: Nope.

NATTER: Well, what *have* you got, Mrs Nitter? I mean, I haven't got all morning.

NITTER: Don't you use that tone of voice with me, Mrs Natter.

NATTER: I'll use whatever tone of voice I like. Now tell me what New Year's resolutions you've got for sale or I'll go somewhere else.

NITTER: You won't get any anywhere else. You'll have to take what's going. (*She produces a box from under the counter and bangs it down*) Here.

NATTER: What's that?

NITTER: It's a 'start being more polite to shopkeepers'.

NATTER: Huh! What else?

NITTER: Didn't think you would cope with that. Well there is this old thing I suppose. (MRS NITTER *pulls a dirty old envelope out of the box. It is covered in dust which she blows all over* MRS NATTER) So sorry. (*She doesn't mean it a bit*)

NATTER: That's quite all right. (*Neither does she*) What is it anyway?

NITTER: Never sold any of them. Been lying around

here for years.

NATTER: Well what *is* it?

NITTER: If you wait a moment we'll see, won't we? (MRS NATTER *taps her fingers impatiently on the counter while* MRS NITTER *puts on her spectacles*)

NATTER: Well?

NITTER: It says here: 'This is a once only, once for all, special offer which is guaranteed to last you a lifetime – and longer.'

NATTER: … 'and longer'?!

NITTER: That's what it says here.

NATTER: Longer than a lifetime? It must be a fake. Where's the catch?

NITTER: It says: 'This, then, is what I command you: love one another.'

NATTER: 'Love one another'? You've got to be joking. That's an impossible resolution.

NITTER: Well it says here: 'If you ask for anything in my name, I will do it.'

NATTER: Whose name? What's it mean? I don't need any help in keeping my resolutions – bloomin' cheek!

NITTER: Well, it goes on: 'You can do nothing without me.'

NATTER: Oh, listen. This is stupid. All I want is to buy my annual packet of New Year's resolutions and you dig out some crazy special offer that says you can have anything you want so long as it's done in the maker's name but at the same time you can't do a blind thing without the maker's help anyway!

NITTER: Well, that's what it says.

NATTER: When was it brought out then, this special offer?

NITTER: Um … let's see … here we are. Two thousand years ago.

NATTER: Two thousand years ago? Probably gone out of business by now. It's way out of date.

NITTER: Not according to this. The sell-by date is Armageddon. And it says: 'Heaven and earth will pass away, but my words will never pass away.'

NATTER: Whose words are they? Who brought out this special offer, then?

NITTER: Um ... (*Looking on the side of the box*) God.

NATTER: God?

NITTER: And Son Ltd.

NATTER: God and Son Ltd?

NITTER: That's what it says: God and Son Ltd.

NATTER: Is there an address?

NITTER: Nope.

NATTER: Well, that's no use, is it? I mean, if you can't even get in touch with the maker?

NITTER: Well, it says here: 'If you love me, you will keep my word, and my Father will love you and we will come to you and make our home with you.'

NATTER: Do what?! I've got a house full of problems as it is. The one thing I *don't* need is a washed-up, out-of-date New Year's resolution company squatting in my front room. I've got quite enough to suffer without all that, thank you very much!

NITTER: But Mrs Natter, it does say here: 'The world will make you suffer. But be of good cheer. I have overcome the world.'

NATTER: 'Be of good cheer'?! Huh! Christmas is over, dear. I'm past all that. I don't care how many promises this God and Son makes, they're not coming to live with me.

NITTER: No.

NATTER: Where do they think they're gonna sleep?!

NITTER: Quite.

NATTER: I mean, really, Mrs Nitter – I haven't the room!

NITTER: Who has, these days?

NATTER: Exactly!

NITTER: Just the bread and the frozen peas then, Mrs Natter? No New Year's resolutions today then?

NATTER: Well there's no point in having what you can't keep, is there, Mrs Nitter?

NITTER: S'pose not.

NATTER: Goodbye then.

NITTER: Goodbye. See you next week.

NATTER: If I survive that long. Cheerio. (MRS NATTER *exits.* MRS NITTER *looks at the envelope and then throws it in the waste bin*)

Talking Heads
by Nigel Forde

TARQUIN CORDELIA ULRICH RICHARD

This has proved to be one of Riding Lights' most popular and useful sketches for all ages and in all situations. It parodies the familiar and interminable television discussions on religious topics with the one obvious difference; that the obligatory Christian on the panel is more quick-witted and articulate than those who are arguing against him – a state of affairs which is all too seldom seen. How often are we going to be obliged to watch those who claim to know the truth about God and the universe reduced to tongue-tied and quivering jellies while vast reserves of ignorance and prejudice are aired with convincing illogicality?

ULRICH, a German Professor, should be leonine and untidy. He sprawls at ease. DAME CORDELIA is of the broken-glass voice and spectacles on strings variety. The interviewer is what we all know interviewers to be. RICHARD FERNHURST should be quick, charming and intelligent. Some of his retorts and some of his questions can appear to be snide or sarcastic; they should simply be logical inferences and it is their logic and not any attitude on the part of the speaker which puts people on the spot.

If this sketch is performed as part of an evening of sketches the chances are that some of the actors involved will need to change before being ready for this one. This difficulty can be overcome by introducing a fifth character, that of the TV floor manager who can set the chairs, check TARQUIN'S make-up, etc. and seat the panel members in the studio as they are ready. This can be improvised in rehearsal until a brief, workable format is arrived at. The floor-manager then calls for silence in the studio and cues the music. Typical music for this kind of programme would be an Albinoni Oboe Concerto or a Corelli Concerto Grosso.

TARQUIN, the interviewer, and his three guests – RICHARD on his right, ULRICH and then DAME CORDELIA on his left – are seated in a semi-circle round a low coffee table with glasses of water. As the lights come up the music fades.

TARQUIN: Good evening. Earlier this evening our
magazine programme 'Stalemate' was tackl-
ing the question 'What Is A Christian?'
Watching that programme and ready to
discuss it now, we have a team of experts
from various fields: Dame Cordelia Verity
from the field of Literature and the History
of Ideas.

CORDELIA: (*With a suave smile to the cameras*) Hello!

TARQUIN: Professor Ulrich von Stadtszentrum-
Einbahnstrasse from the field of Experimen-
tal Theology and Anthropocentralism.

ULRICH: Gut eefning!

TARQUIN: And Mr Richard Fernhurst from a field of
dairy cattle and mangold-wurzels.

RICHARD: Good evening.

TARQUIN: Let's start with Professor Ulrich von
Stadtszentrum-Einbahnstrasse. Ully – what
impressed you about the programme?

ULRICH: (*After a moment's thought, polishing his
glasses*) Nossing.

TARQUIN: Could you ... could you perhaps expand that
a little?

ULRICH: Oh yes. (*There is silence*)

TARQUIN: *Would* you perhaps expand that a little?

ULRICH: Well, I voz very disappointed that there voz
no exploration into der qvestion 'Is der, in
fect, any evidence of a soul as distinct from a
body?' Instead ve are faced viz all dese
fetuous arguments from pipple who assume
der spiritual part of man ven der is no anatom-
ical evidence vatsoeffer. Shouldn't it?

TARQUIN: Are you, in fact, saying that if we cut somebody open, if we vivisected somebody, we
could prove or disprove Christianity?

CORDELIA: (*Smoothly confident*) Well, this is nonsense,
isn't it? Christianity is to be found entirely in
the emotions and the imagination if it is to be
found anywhere; and you're not going to be
able to pinpoint the imagination among all
those horrid gristly bits, are you?

RICHARD: Just a minute – aren't we getting rather a
long way from the actual programme that we
saw?

CORDELIA: (*Pityingly*) Well, of course! We're criticising it.

TARQUIN: Richard? Can I bring you in here?

RICHARD: Yes, thank you. You see, I thought the most interesting bits of the programme were where they were quoting what seemed to me very important and relevant passages from the Bible itself.

CORDELIA: (*Coldly*) Oh, you find that interesting, do you?

RICHARD: (*Taking the question seriously*) Well, it did bring us back to the facts about Christianity, and facts are much more important than one or two people's whimsical and highly personal opinions.

TARQUIN: But the programme was trying to find out what a Christian is.

RICHARD: Exactly. And you don't do that by agreeing with anyone's guess. You do it in the same way as you'd find out about anything: you find out what various examples have in common, not where they are different.

CORDELIA: (*On her hobby-horse*) Well, I'm a writer ..

RICHARD: Fine! What is a writer? It's someone who writes.(ULRICH *shakes his head and makes 'hehyeyeyeyey' noises gently to himself, indicative of the supreme intellectual effort needed to follow this train of thought*) He or she may be moral or immoral, tall, short, happy, successful, anything you like, but the point is that it is someone who writes.

ULRICH: Vot, may I ask, hez dis to do viz Christiennity?

CORDELIA: Exactly! A Christian, surely, is someone who tries to lead a good life. That's it in a nutshell.

RICHARD: Do you really think so? I mean, you wouldn't call yourself a Christian, would you? I know you've written a lot against it, and yet you'd be the first to say that you led a good life, as far as you could.

ULRICH: (*who has been trying to puzzle this one out*) Vot ... er ... vot is dis Nuttschell?

TARQUIN: Please, Ully ...

CORDELIA: (*Slightly ruffled*) Yes. Well, of course ... no ... what I mean is ... a Christian is obviously not just someone who leads a good life, but, er ... someone who goes to church!

RICHARD: I've met a lot of people who go to church and have no belief in Jesus Christ whatsoever.

CORDELIA: (*Taking any chance to be withering*) Oh, so have I! (*Suddenly realises that this has completely destroyed her point*) Yes … yes … I mean, they go to church, and they're good people and though they … though they don't believe in Jesus Christ, they do believe that there is a God. Yes. That's it! A Christian believes in God.

RICHARD: So the Devil is a Christian?

ULRICH: (*Suddenly with us again*) Ahhhhh! Zis is very interesting!

CORDELIA: What do you mean, 'the Devil is a Christian'?

ULRICH: (*Muttering*) What do you mean 'the Devil is a Christian'?

RICHARD: Well, he believes in God. He's got plenty of reason to!

CORDELIA: That doesn't make him a Christian!

RICHARD: Ah, so a Christian isn't just someone who believes in God?

CORDELIA: (*Slightly desperately*) No, no, not *just* someone who believes in God. No.

TARQUIN: Just a minute, Richard. Are you saying that a Christian is not necessarily moral, good, someone who goes to church … ?

RICHARD: I am saying that they might be, but that's not what makes them Christians. Cordelia might be good at punctuation and spelling, but that isn't what makes her a writer. I'm good at punctuation and spelling, but I'm not a writer.

ULRICH: (*He takes it slowly to make sure he's got it right*) So … so now, we can recognise der Christian from vere he puts his semi-colon?

TARQUIN: Oh, shut u– thank you, Ully.

RICHARD: A Christian is someone who believes and trusts in Jesus Christ and bases his life on him.

CORDELIA: (*Scathingly*) That's rather old-fashioned, isn't it?

RICHARD: So's breathing but it still works.

TARQUIN: (*Stepping in hastily*) Well, we could talk all night but we shall have to leave it there, I'm afraid.

ULRICH: Ah, so now ve hef der Christian full stop!
TARQUIN: Yes. Thank you, Ully. Until next week at the
same time, goodbye.
(*Music comes in*)
ULRICH: Punkt, eh? I crack der yolk, ja?

(*The lights fade*)

Do unto Others ...
by Paul Burbridge

GORDON, *a professional man who exudes the easy confidence which comes from success*   JENNIFER, *his wife, capable yet reserved*   MARTIN, *a lonely neighbour*

For those whose lives run comparatively smoothly it is often difficult to sympathise genuinely with the problems many people encounter; harder still to allow one's privacy to be invaded and to become involved in practical help. Within Christian circles, outright rejection is rare, though cheery words of encouragement can amount to the same thing. The Epistle of James has much to say about those who tell the needy to 'Go in peace, be warmed and filled.' This sketch can challenge all of us to show the fruit of the Spirit in very practical ways to alleviate the suffering of others.

The scene takes place in the comfort of GORDON *and* JENNIFER's *lounge. They have obviously just settled down for a quiet evening;* GORDON *with some autobiography or other,* JENNIFER *with her embroidery. The doorbell rings. Neither responds. After a pause,* JENNIFER *casts an irritated look at* GORDON, *sighs and leaves the room. From offstage we hear the door open and Jennifer say without enthusiasm:*

JENNIFER: Oh, hullo, Martin. How nice to see you. Do you want to come in?

MARTIN: Yes, please, that would be very nice.

JENNIFER: (*Leading* MARTIN *into the lounge*) Gordon, darling, Martin's here.

GORDON: Oh, is he? (*Then realising that* MARTIN *is in the room, he leaps up and says hastily*) Oh, er, what a surprise.

MARTIN: I thought I'd just pop in and see how you were and ...

GORDON: Did you?

MARTIN: I won't stay long, I ...

GORDON: Good.

JENNIFER: Do sit yourself down, Martin.

GORDON: (*With exaggerated bonhomie*) Yes, please.

Come on in. Welcome. Have a seat.

MARTIN: Thank you. This one? (*He begins to sit down*)

GORDON: Well, er, Jennifer was sitting there, but, um … no, no, no, yes, please sit down.

JENNIFER: I'll make some coffee. Coffee, Martin?

MARTIN: Please.

GORDON: (*Beaming*) Jennifer will make some coffee. (*Exit* JENNIFER) So, how's life then, Martin? Things ticking over all right?

MARTIN: Well, no, I can't say they are actually, Gordon.

GORDON: I know what you mean. I've had a desperate week myself. The office has been positively crawling with people groaning about this, that or the other. Always something, isn't there?

MARTIN: Hmmm. Yes.

GORDON: (*Blustering*) Still, life goes on and there we are. At least we can cheer one another up.

MARTIN: I'm certainly very grateful to be able to come in for a chat. I've been feeling rather lonely recently.

GORDON: I wonder what's happened to that coffee? Ah! Here we are. (*Enter* JENNIFER *with tray of coffee*) That's it.

JENNIFER: (*Serving the coffee*) White, Martin? It's two, isn't it?

MARTIN: Yes, thank you.

GORDON: (*With patronising authority*) Now, how do you like your coffee, Martin? Sugar?

JENNIFER: (*Testily*) It's all right, thank you, Gordon.

GORDON: Oh, I see you've got it. That's fine. So long as you're all right. (*He remains standing to drink his coffee*)

JENNIFER: How are you these days, Martin?

MARTIN: Well, I was just telling Gordon that I haven't been feeling so good recently. I suppose that being out of work for so long hasn't helped matters, and there have been one or two other problems with the …

GORDON: There really is so much unemployment about these days. Only last night there was a whole documentary about it on the television. We didn't see all of it.

MARTIN: I know, I couldn't watch it.

JENNIFER: (*Feeling the need to be kindly*) Are there no jobs advertised which you could consider, Martin?

MARTIN: Not many. Without a car, you see, anything more than a couple of miles away is extremely difficult and anyway the whole thing is complicated by the fact ...

JENNIFER: *Do* you drive?

MARTIN: Yes, I do, but sales reps' cars are normally provided by the firm.

GORDON: (*Pleasantly*) What firm do you work for?

JENNIFER: Martin hasn't got a job at the moment, Gordon.

GORDON: Hasn't he? Oh.

MARTIN: No.

GORDON: No, of course you haven't. Silly of me. I did know that.

JENNIFER: Isn't there something which you could be doing in the meantime to keep yourself occupied? Part-time work or anything?

MARTIN: I've been thinking about that. I've done a few odd jobs round the house and I've been reading a bit.

GORDON: (*Seizing upon a moment of contact*) *Watership Down*'s a good book. So, er, Jennifer was saying. It's all about rats.

JENNIFER: Rabbits.

GORDON: Rabbits. That's it. (*Pause*) You should read it.

MARTIN: I have.

GORDON: Good. (*Silence*)

MARTIN: The trouble is nothing seems to take my mind off things at the moment. I'm not *that* worried about the work. Something'll turn up sooner or later. My real worry at the moment ... I don't know whether I should tell anyone yet ... because it hasn't been confirmed. Well, I saw my doctor the other day ...

JENNIFER: Was it something he said?

MARTIN: Sort of. It was more what he didn't say, really.

GORDON: Not been a hundred per cent recently?

JENNIFER: Nothing serious, I hope, Martin?

MARTIN: I hope not. I really do. He wouldn't say. He just said I'd have to go in for a series of tests and X-rays and things.

JENNIFER: Oh, dear.

MARTIN: I may be being stupid. It may all be nothing, but I just keep wondering if I've got … you know …

GORDON: More coffee?

MARTIN: The tests will all be done on …

GORDON: (*With sudden inspiration*) Tea? Nice cup of tea?

MARTIN: Lots of people have tests, don't they?

GORDON: (*Concealing his desperation behind a smile*) We can get you a cold drink if you'd prefer it?

MARTIN: (*Who has been oblivious to* GORDON*'s offers*) Just because you go in for a test doesn't mean there's anything wrong, does it, Jennifer?

JENNIFER: Oh, I don't think so. I'm sure it'll just be a routine check-up, that's all.

MARTIN: (*Genuinely distressed*) Do you think so?

JENNIFER: I'm sure. It's good to have a check-up now and again. (*There follows an uneasy silence*)

MARTIN: Well, I suppose I'd better not keep you up.

GORDON: You've got transport, then?

JENNIFER: (*Inwardly cringing*) I think it would be nice if you gave Martin a lift home, Gordon.

GORDON: Certainly, anything, yes. My car's just outside. Okaaay! (*With a final thin veneer of heartiness*) You all right then, Martin?

MARTIN: (*Quietly*) Yes, thanks. I'm fine. (*He follows* GORDON *out*)

A Man After My Own
by Nigel Forde

HUSBAND WIFE LOVER

Stylisation does not mean unreality. Stylisation is one theatrical method of achieving reality; a deeper reality than mere naturalism would give. This sketch is stylised, but that is a mere matter of form: the content must be emotionally direct and truthful. The stylisation lies in the telling juxtaposition of what we hear, not in the content of the lines.

When this sketch was produced as part of The Vanity Case *the* HUSBAND *and* WIFE *stood in two separate metal structures rather like cages – a visual metaphor for their attitudes towards their marriage – while the* LOVER *was free to move about the stage. At the end the* WIFE *was stepping out of the cage (but never quite did so) to join him. Another way of doing it is for the* HUSBAND *and* WIFE, *as they speak the first two speeches, to be engaged in doing something trivially diurnal such as final preparations for going out – tying shoelaces, brushing jacket, putting on make-up. Actors will, I hope, find their own way of providing a natural and helpful counterpoint to their spoken thoughts.*

The LOVER *should not appear until just before his first line so that he becomes an extra dimension to the sketch rather than what the sketch is all about.*

Just as the optimist says 'the bottle is half-full' and the pessimist says 'the bottle is half-empty', so the HUSBAND *and* WIFE *virtually the same things but betray, by the way they express themselves, their different hopes and expectations. The* LOVER *undercuts both of them. It will help the sketch if this structure is kept in mind.*

HUSBAND: Linda and I have been married for eight and a half years. Of course, our marriage isn't perfect, but it's too late now to change our minds. I mean, whose marriage is perfect? No, we've just got to go on as best we can. My wife is still very attractive and we've got two lovely children. It's just a matter of putting our minds to it – surely we're intelligent enough

to make it work? Marriage is an awful lot
more than just sex. After all, when it comes
down to it, a promise is a promise.

WIFE: I married John nearly nine years ago. Our
marriage is far from ideal, but it's almost too
late now to change our minds. I mean, some
people seem to be happy; I suppose we just
have to go on as best we can. I hope other
men still find me attractive. The children are
a problem, but I suppose it's just a matter of
seeing how things go. I hope we're mature
enough to face facts. Well. I suppose marriage isn't *just* sex. But I didn't know what I
was promising at the time. How could I?

HUSBAND: Linda and I have been married for eight and
a half years.
WIFE: I married John nearly nine years ago.
LOVER: Do you realise, you've stuck it for almost ten
years so far?

HUSBAND: Of course, our marriage isn't perfect.
WIFE: Our marriage is far from ideal.
LOVER: Of course, you two should never have got
married.

HUSBAND: It's too late now to change our minds.
WIFE: It's almost too late now to change our minds.
LOVER: It's never too late to change your mind …

HUSBAND· I mean, whose marriage is perfect?
WIFE: I mean, some people seem to be happy.
LOVER: You owe it to yourself to be happy.

HUSBAND: We've got to go on as best we can.
WIFE: I suppose we just have to go on as best we
can.
LOVER: You can't go on like this.

HUSBAND: My wife is still very attractive.
WIFE: I hope other men still find me attractive.
LOVER: An attractive girl like you …

HUSBAND: We've got two lovely children.
WIFE: The children are a problem.

LOVER: It's a pity about the kids, but there you are.

HUSBAND: It's just a matter of putting our minds to it.
WIFE: I suppose it's just a matter of seeing how things go.
LOVER: It's what you feel, now, that matters.

HUSBAND: We're intelligent enough to make it work.
WIFE: I hope we're mature enough to face facts.
LOVER: You're not kids any more: you know when you're beaten.

HUSBAND: I mean, marriage is an awful lot more than just sex.
WIFE: I suppose marriage isn't *just* sex.
LOVER: I mean, take sex away from marriage – what have you got left?

HUSBAND: After all, when it comes down to it, a promise is a promise.
WIFE: I didn't know what ı was promising at the time; how could I?
LOVER: It's not your fault: everyone breaks promises. (*Pause*) Let me take care of you.
WIFE: *Will* you take care of me?
LOVER: I promise.

(*Fast fade to blackout*)

Using Your Loaf
by Nigel Forde

*The technique of performing this sketch is the same as that for
100% PROOF (see p.19). There is one difference: in 100%
PROOF, the telephone was very much a vehicle for listening to
what Hymie had to say and John contributes very little apart from
the fact that he is there to talk to. In this sketch quite a bit of the
humour is based on what Mum is presumed to be saying at the other
end of the line. We can only imagine and understand that by the little BOY's replies, so a slightly more developed telephone technique
has to be worked out and time given for Mum to say what she has
to. This telephone should, of course, be a public one and maybe
there are opportunities for the BOY to have to insert more money at
crucial stages of the conversation. Each actor and director will be
able to work out his own descant, as it were, to the supplied text.*

A SMALL BOY *is on the telephone to his mother. It is immediately
after Jesus's feeding of the five thousand ...*

BOY: Hallo? ... Hallo? Mum? ... Yes, I know I
should have been home over an hour ago ...
I'm sorry; I won't be long now. Mum, it's ...
er ... it's about that list you gave me ... yes ...
I'm afraid I couldn't get Dad's paper; they'd
sold out. But tell him Ramoth-Gilead are
still top of the division, and they meet Gilgal
in the next round of the Milk and Honey Cup
... Right? ... Now ...
(*He produces his list*) You've got down here
'eight barley loaves and eight fillets of plaice'
... that's right ... On the – er – on the loaves
... apparently there's been a bit of a rush for
the wholemeal foods after all this cholesterol
scare, you know, and he only had five left ...
is that O.K.? ... And I didn't have much joy
on the fish front either. He said that some
bloke went out fishing last week, caught
nothing, and then, suddenly, on his last go
he cleared the whole flippin' lake! Bust his
nets, though! ... Yeah, it does serve him

right! ... Anyway, I just got a couple of
ten-ounce mackerel ... I *know*, but that's all
there was ... Yes! Oh, yes! ... I mean, five
loaves and two little fishes *is* better than
nothing ... sure it was – *is*! ... Only, look,
Mum ... I don't quite know how to tell you
this ... only, a funny thing happened to me
on the way to ... no, no; not funny-ha-ha,
funny-peculiar. You remember Simon and
Andrew? ... Yes, you do! Simon was a big
bloke ... muscular, always shootin' his
mouth off ... Used to fish ... No, no – not he
was used to fish – he used to fish ... He was a
fisherman ... Well, of course a fisherman
would be used to f— look, Mum, forget it.
You know who I'm talkin' about? Well, I've
just bumped into his brother ... eh? ... well,
they were *both* fishermen ... Andrew *and*
Simon. Only now he's called Peter. No, not
Andrew – Simon. Yes, Andrew's still called
Andrew ... No ... he doesn't any more ... I
would have asked him for some fish if he'd
still been a fisherman, but it was ... well, it
was sort of the other way round, really. Yes
... he asked me for my two mackerel ... that's
right ... no, no – both of them, both ... um ...
mackerel ... and the five loaves. Now Mum,
listen! *Please*! Just listen, Mum ... Yes, they
have ... Well I wouldn't say 'gone all religious' but, yes, it is a religious sort of thing ...
You thought they ate *what*?? Really??? ...
He never said anything to me about locusts
... or wild honey – just bread and fish ... I
should have asked to see who? Oh, well,
they took me to the man at the top anyway ...
Jesus ... no, it was definitely Jesus ... he was
the one who wanted the bread and the fish in
the first place ... I couldn't refuse, really,
could I? I mean, put yourself in my position
– what would you have said? (*There is a long
pause while he listens*) Well ... perhaps it's
just as well you weren't in my position then
... Honestly, Mum, I couldn't say no – he
was so nice about it ... yes, but then you
haven't met him, have you? ... What did he

want what for? ... Oh, well, they'd all come
out without any packed lunch or anything ...
Mmm? ... Yes, there *are* twelve ... thirteen
including Jesus ... (*Laughing*) Oh, no, no,
no! He wasn't thinking of trying to make five
loaves and two fishes go round thirteen
people! Oh, goodness me, no! ... Mmm?
Oh, five thousand ... (*Something has happened at the other end*) Mum? ... MUM???
... Are you all right? ... I know, it's a very
hard floor, yes ... no, Mum, I *wasn't*
exaggerating again, really I wasn't. Well – I
was a bit; four thousand nine hundred and
ninety-nine – one of them wasn't hungry ...
Because I counted them, that's how ... Yes,
of course you can make mistakes counting
that many heads. That's why I did it the
simple way ... eh? ... You count the arms
and legs and divide by four ... Yes, I'm sorry,
it was ... yes – 'flippant' is a very good word
for it ... But does it really matter how many?
I mean, there's an awful lot of people here ...
No, I don't think it's anything officially to do
with the synagogue – mind you, there's a lot
of sinners agog here! I say! There's a lot of
yes I'm sorry, it was, wasn't it ... What? ...
Yes, they were! ... Mum, I realise you're
finding this difficult to believe, but they were
all fed. Everyone had as much as he wanted
... Except who? ... Ah – yes ... Well, couldn't
we just have – um – a nice glass of water and
a fig? ... I *have* got some money left, but the
shops are all closed now ... No ... no, it
didn't cross my mind to ask for anything in
return ... I mean, from what I'd heard about
Jesus, I didn't think he was the sort to take
advantage of – hang on just a second, Mum.
(*Someone offstage is trying to tell him something*)
There's what? Eh? For *me*? ... Twelve!!! Yes
... Yes ... Four of fish and eight of bread ...
(*Back to the telephone*) Mum, I wonder if I
could borrow the horse and cart? ... I *was*
thinking about tea, yes. What about Eli and
Rebecca? ... No, not borrowing *from*,

inviting *to*. Yes ... well, I think I've found a solution. (*Smiles to disciple offstage*) Her uncle? Is he? And four kids and her sister-in-law. That's O.K.: they can come too. And we could ask Daniel and Miriam and that nice man at number fifteen, and Jemuel and his brother ...

(*Lights begin to fade*)

Oh, and Benjamin and Judith with their kids. Susannah, of course, and it's about time we had Samuel round ...

(*Blackout*)

Life Is But a Melancholy Flower
by Nigel Forde

DAFFODIL ONE   DAFFODIL TWO

I'm not sure where this sketch had its origins. Perhaps there is a vague influence from the story of the seed which has to be put into the ground and die before it can live; perhaps it was the fact that talk about life after death (along with whether Adam and Eve are literally true or myths, and the reliability of the Biblical records) is a favourite pagan launching pad against the faith.

After all, we can see, as humans, that daffodils do die and then live again. Perhaps, a step further up the biological ladder, someone knows something similar about humans, which we, earthbound as we are, cannot see.

An Easter sketch, perhaps. Certainly a sketch which can arouse discussion in an evangelistic context. Without doubt one which can be performed by an all-female cast – there, at least, is a novelty.

The ideal setting for this would be a painted groundrow of grasses and plants behind which the daffodils can stand. Daffodil headdresses of not too painful construction are necessary. Green leotards would be wonderful. A gentle background noise of birdsong and distant lambs bleating would complete the idyll.

DAFFODIL 1: (Musing) When I come back ... I'd like to come back as a primrose.

DAFFODIL 2: D'jer what, Daff?

DAFFODIL 1: Yes, that's it. As a primrose!

DAFFODIL 2: Come back when?

DAFFODIL 1: You know!

DAFFODIL 2: No?

DAFFODIL 1: After.

DAFFODIL 2: After?

DAFFODIL 1: After I've crossed over. Passed away. Gone to join the Great Seed Merchant in the Skies.

DAFFODIL 2 Oh! When you've snuffed it!

DAFFODIL 1. (*Slightly shocked at such an indelicate phrase*) Yes, dear.

DAFFODIL 2 Well, you won't be coming back, will you?

Anyway, I wouldn't want to be a primrose.
Why a primrose?

DAFFODIL 1: Well, they've got lovely little runnels on
their leaves, haven't they? Keep the water
off your stem.

DAFFODIL 2: Keeping the water off your stem's not everything.

DAFFODIL 1: (*Sarcastically*) Oh! Oh, really! We have a
philosopher in our midst, have we? (*Blackly*)
That Wordsworth's got a lot to answer for:
one mention in one poem and she thinks
she's a star!

DAFFODIL 2: (*Preening herself*) I've been anthologised!

DAFFODIL 1: Yeah, well – that's a new word for it!

DAFFODIL 2: Oh, come on! Look, don't let's quarrel! It's
just that I don't see the point in dreaming
about another life after death. Three score
days and ten – that's our allotted span, and
that's it!

DAFFODIL 1: (*Pause, then diffidently*) Don't you believe in
perennials, then?

DAFFODIL 2: Perennials? Don't make me laugh! You can
talk till you've crumpled your corolla, but
you won't change my mind. We're all annu-
als. When we're finished, we're finished!

DAFFODIL 1: But … when we die …

DAFFODIL 2: Yes?

DAFFODIL 1: Well, surely there's a part of us, a corm, a
bulb, call it what you will, that lives on?

DAFFODIL 2: Where did you learn all that rubbish? Have
you ever seen your bulb? Well? Go on – have
you?

DAFFODIL 1: Well, no, but …

DAFFODIL 2: Well, there you are then. All this super-
natural nonsense! When the farmer came in
the other day and did … well, what he did …
to little Violet, did you see any corm, any
bulb?

DAFFODIL 1: (*Realising she's on shaky ground*) Well – no,
I won't lie to you; I didn't. But I've always
been brought up to believe that with us
daffodils it's different. That we'll have
another life; that it's *not* the end, because
we've got a bulb.

DAFFODIL 2: But why should we be any different from all

the others?

DAFFODIL 1: Oh, it's not just us! Crocuses as well – snow-drops – and tulips.

DAFFODIL 2: (*Can't believe what she's hearing*) Tulips? Tulips??? You don't really believe in *tulips*, do you? *Cultivated* flowers! Go on!

DAFFODIL 1: (*Uncomfortably*) I didn't say I believed in them …

DAFFODIL 2: You'll be telling me next you believe in vegetables!

DAFFODIL 1: Oh, come off it! All I'm saying …

DAFFODIL 2: (*As if shouting 'demons' and 'ghosties'*) Artichokes!!! Parsnips!!! PURPLE SPROUTING BROCCOLIEEEAAGGGHHHH!!!!!!

DAFFODIL 1: Oh, look! Don't be daft, Reen, of course I don't believe in all them, but that doesn't mean we haven't got a bulb, does it?

DAFFODIL 2: You know what, Daff. You're nave.

DAFFODIL 1: What?

DAFFODIL 2: Nave. It's a French word meaning 'simple and believing'.

DAFFODIL 1: Oh, here we go! Just 'cos your mum got picked by Interflora …

DAFFODIL 2: Well, that's it, Daff. You've got to have ambition. Live while you can. No point in banking on corms and bulbs and having a second chance.

DAFFODIL 1: Unless it's true, of course …

DAFFODIL 2: Well, let's agree to differ, eh? Now excuse me while I comb me calyx and powder me pistils.

DAFFODIL 1: What for?

DAFFODIL 2: The photographer of course!

DAFFODIL 1: Eh?

DAFFODIL 2: He's coming to snap me.

DAFFODIL 1: Reen, he's not! You're not … you're not going to be gathered!

DAFFODIL 2: No, no. Snap me – take me picture! Put me on an Easter card with a little lamb and a chicken's egg. I'll be famous! I'll be celeb-rated! I'll be immortal!

DAFFODIL 1: You'll probably be creased up the middle where the card bends.

DAFFODIL 2: At least I'll have done something with my life, not just wasted my sweetness on the desert air.

DAFFODIL 1: Yeah ... I s'pose you will,. D'you *really* not
believe in corms and bulbs?

DAFFODIL 2: It's a very pretty story, but we're not seed-
lings any longer, you know.

DAFFODIL 1: No. (*Searching for a crumb of comfort*)
Trees! There could be such things as trees,
you know! Like us, but huge, and living for
years and years!

(*Lights begin to fade*)

Or ivy, which can live through the winter and
doesn't ever have any blossom! I mean,
what's your position on rhizomes?

(*Blackout*)

A GUIDE TO MORALITY PLAYS

What is a morality play?

Morality plays were first performed in the Middle Ages, although their ancestry can be traced back to ancient times. They differ from the mystery (or miracle) plays in several respects. The mystery plays are really the forerunners of the biblical sketches that we perform in our churches today. They were principally concerned with the actual events and characters of the biblical narrative, even when they included a great deal of comic invention. Whole cycles of short plays, performed by different guilds, combined to tell the story of salvation from The Creation to The Last Judgement. The morality plays were a later development. They were more like illustrated sermons than illustrated Bible stories. Like a powerful preacher, a successful morality play held sway over its audience, inviting the sinner to shun evil and to embrace the truth. Such plays had an emotional appeal, particularly in an age when life expectancy was short and the church emphasised the terrors of hell.

Characters in morality plays typify virtues and vices: 'Sloth', 'Ignorance', 'Chastity', 'Good Works'. Central characters often represent humanity, as with 'Everyman' and 'Mankind'. Good angels and bad angels appear, offering their advice to the human soul, which struggles in the conflict between righteousness and sin, God and the Devil. The outcome is characteristically a happy ending, even if a sober one: Mankind repents and turns to God at the hour of his death.

Most morality plays, not surprisingly, had a very serious tone. Perhaps this is the reason why the tradition has been neglected in recent years, whilst the mystery plays have enjoyed many notable revivals. Yet there is a great richness in the morality tradition which is well worth discovering.

The Bible and the Early Church

The principal feature of the morality play, the personification of ideas, can be found in the Bible. In Genesis 4, Cain is warned by God: 'Sin is crouching at the door; its desire is for you, but you must have the mastery.' Here, sin is characterised as an animal, lying in wait for its prey. Another example is the personification of wisdom in Proverbs 8: 'On the height beside the way, in the path she takes her stand ... Wisdom is better than jewels, all that you desire cannot compare with her ... I, wisdom, dwell in prudence, and I find knowledge and discretion ... The Lord created me at the beginning of his work.' Proverbs 14 characterises folly as a destroyer of wisdom: 'Wisdom builds her house, but folly with her own hands tears it down.' Perhaps the most graphic personification of all, and certainly influential on the minds of medieval artists and writers, is the portrayal of death in Revelation 6: 'When he opened the fourth seal, I heard the voice of the fourth living creature say "Come!" And I saw, and behold, a pale horse, and its rider's name was Death, and Hades followed him; and they were given power over a fourth of the earth, to kill with the sword and with famine and with pestilence and by wild beasts of the earth.' To say that this is a personification of death does not undermine the literal terror of this prophecy: the image helps us to see the truth more vividly.

The same device is used by a number of early Christian writers. One of the most notable antecedents of the morality play is the work of the Christian Latin poet Prudentius. At the end of the fourth century, he wrote an allegory called the *Psychomachia* (Battle for the Human Soul). The virtues enter the lists with the vices in a succession of jousts, each virtue achieving victory. In another allegory, called the *Hamartigenia* (The Origin of Sin), the soul is depicted as a fortress and assailed by the Devil with an army of vices, who act as tempters. In this case, the vices win and the human race is held in thrall. Prudentius' work was a favourite with Christian artists in the centuries to come.

Two medieval morality plays

The earliest complete morality play in the English language is *The Castell of Perseverance*, written about 1425. Not only the lengthy text of 3,600 lines has survived, but also the stage directions and the set design. The play was staged in the round, with a central tower representing the castle, surrounded by a circular moat and five scaffolds severally labelled 'Flesh', 'World', 'Belial', 'Covetousness' and 'God'. Pageantry and colour-symbolism played a great part. 'The four daughters shall be clad in mantles, Mercy in white, Righteousness in red altogether, Truth in sad green and Peace in black and they shall play in the place all together till they bring up the soul.' From simple details such as these, we can see that the earliest morality plays were highly stylized. The staging, the costumes and the personification of virtues and vices all contributed to a didactic purpose. Yet even a solemn play like this was much more than a sermon in pictures. There were stage effects with gunpowder, a moat filled with water, dramatic duels, music, and some memorable theatrical inventions. The virtues, for instance, are armed with red roses, symbolising Christ's passion. Wrath falls to the ground, crying: 'I am beten blak and blo with a rose that on rode was rent' (I am beaten black and blue with a rose that was torn on the cross). The plot of *The Castell of Perseverance* is characteristic of many morality plays. Mankind is seen on a journey from birth to death. Along the way, virtues and vices war for his soul. Repenting of his worldliness, he is escorted to a bastion of security, the castle, where he is protected against the assaults of the Devil. However, Covetousness lures him away to the false security of materialism. Death arrives and strips him of all his possessions. The soul of Mankind is then conducted to hell. At this point, Mercy, Truth, Righteousness and Peace debate over Mankind's eternal destiny; Mercy and Peace pleading for leniency, Truth and Righteousness demanding judgement. They take their case to God, who decides in favour of Mercy and Peace. Mankind is saved by the atoning blood of Christ.

The most famous morality play of all is *Everyman*, written about 1500. The preface declares: 'Here beginneth a treatise how the High Father of Heaven sendeth Death to summon every creature to come and give account of their lives in this world, and is in manner of a moral play.' *Everyman* is a very short play and is often published in collections of medieval plays. It is well worth buying a copy or borrowing it from a library, to see how a classic morality play works. Here, it is sufficient to say that God sends Death to summon Everyman. Everyman tries to find companions to go on his journey but Fellowship, Kindred and Goods refuse to accompany him. Everyman faces his final journey alone. Only Good Deeds can assist him, but she is too weak to stand up. Her sister Knowledge arrives and leads Everyman to Confession. He does penance and thereby restores Good Deeds to health. Wearing the robe of contrition, he is joined by Discretion, Strength, Five Wits and Beauty; and is now ready for the last sacrament. Finally facing death, Everyman is deserted by all except Good Deeds and Knowledge. He sinks into his grave and Knowledge declares that Everyman's soul will be received by God. A doctor enters and solemnly warns the spectators to amend their lives before it is too late.

John Bunyan and the morality tradition

Morality and mystery plays were stamped out at the height of their popularity. Their pre-reformation theology and their association with public festivals, and – in the case of the mystery plays – frequently with ribald comedy, did no' appeal to the austere Puritans. The theatre and the church were held to have little in common and so, ironically, the performance of morality plays came to be associated with the lowering of public morality. The end of the sixteenth century saw the last performances of the religious plays of the Middle Ages. At the same time, a new kind of secular theatre was developing which had little interest in the two-dimensional world of the morality play. Echoes remain in Marlowe's *Dr Faustus*, with the appearance of the Seven Deadly Sins, and the comedies of Ben Jonson, where the characters are frequently named after attributes: 'Lovewit'; 'Tribulation'; 'Sir Epicure Mammon'; 'Lady Would-be'; but in both Marlowe and Jonson's case, and particularly in Shakespeare's, the interest centres on the individual character who is more complex than any particular type. Elizabethan and Jacobean theatre brought a psychological realism that was a far greater deathblow to the traditional morality play than the edicts of the Puritans. The morality play no longer satisfied the yearning for rounded human characters in dramas that expressed the religious and social dilemmas of an increasingly complex society.

It was left to an itinerant, nonconformist preacher, called John Bunyan, to revive the spirit of the morality play in the seventeenth century. In 1675 he wrote *The Pilgrim's Progress*, which wedded the evangelical Christianity of Puritan England to the tradition of the Catholic morality play. Whether or not he consciously looked back at the old religious plays, Bunyan chose the literary device which would most clearly present his theological message. The morality tradition is the natural one for a popular preacher: it is unambiguous and leaves no doubt about the author's intentions. Bunyan's moral tale was forthright in its purpose and achieved a simplicity of communication which, with his command of English prose and vivid imagination, earned him a place in the history of English literature. *The Pilgrim's Progress* became one of the greatest influences on Christian piety in Britain. For two centuries it was second only to the Bible in many Christian homes. Although it was not a play, much of *The Pilgrim's Progress* was written simply as dialogue between different characters who represent spiritual types. We meet 'Mr Worldly-Wiseman', 'Faithful', 'Ignorance', 'Talkative', 'Hold-the-World', 'Money-Love', 'Superstition' and 'Hopeful'. The theme of the spiritual journey of mankind is dramatised in the adventures of Christian, who leaves the City of Destruction and heads for the Celestial City, by way of the Cross, the Valley of Humiliation, Vanity Fair and Doubting Castle. Theologically, we are in a very different environment to *Everyman*. Nevertheless, the great morality plays and stories share a universal relevance. The human soul journeys through the trials and temptations of life. All men must face death; none can do so without turning to God for mercy.

The survival of the morality play

We are not concerned here with the morality tradition in novels or satirical comedies, but it is worth mentioning that the disappearance of the morality play has never been total. Popular theatre, particularly the emergence of melodrama in the nineteenth century, has ensured the survival of many familiar elements: stereotypes, the victory of good over evil, a simple plot reinforced by stylization, music and stage effects, all directed towards pointing a moral for the edification of the audience. Typically, Victorian melodrama concentrated on the sexual and social morality of the day. Wicked landlords exploit poor tenants, corrupt noblemen lead innocent girls astray, good men are foully murdered in the pursuit of justice but the villain is apprehended and receives his due punishment. The moral is clear, although frequently the audience has become so involved along the way in the ravishing of the heroine, or the bloody demise of the villain, that the moral has become of decidedly secondary interest. Melodrama originally meant drama with musical accompaniment, and the best Victorian melodrama was performed with appropriate trembles and dramatic chords on the piano.

Despite various tributaries, such as the melodrama, pantomime, silent films, popular Marxist theatre or the 'cops and robbers' movie, where the villain always gets his come-uppance, the traditional morality play (in its strictest religious sense) deserves a comeback. It has scarcely been seen since its heyday, but it has a great deal to offer in the way of popular communication of the gospel.

Introduction to 'Trimmer Trend'

The Trial of Trimmer Trend was originally written for Bread-rock Street Theatre Company. It is a rough and ready piece, which explores a few of the possibilities found in the morality tradition. As well as presenting the play for performance, the idea is to illustrate the sort of experiment that may be worth making.

The sources for a play like this are several. Firstly, the traditional morality plays such as *The Castell of Perseverance* and *Everyman*; secondly, Victorian melodrama and music hall; thirdly, pantomime. Theologically, it is a simple, evangelistic piece, intended to show the need to face up to guilt honestly and to turn to Christ. Some will feel strongly that such a serious purpose can never be conveyed satisfactorily by humour: ideally, that should be an incentive to write more serious morality plays. In this case, it seemed appropriate to the street theatre context of the play to use comedy much more liberally than is normal in morality plays. Laughter, as the title of this book suggests, is as much a heavenly attribute as serious piety. There is a joy in salvation, and the comedy of *The Trial of Trimmer Trend* is to help the audience see the absurdity of running away from one's own conscience and from the Word of God; and to invite them to share in the laughter of release from fear.

Trimmer Trend makes his pilgrimage, a downhill descent towards death and judgement, as he ignores the truth and heeds false counsellors. He is rescued only by turning to the cross at the eleventh hour. This is the serious climax of the play, and the mime should be treated with dignity. It is a simple, direct and sober illustration of how Christ bears our sins upon the cross. The epilogue to the play returns to comedy, just as the Resurrection brings joy to the disciples after the Crucifixion; and, in the way of all morality plays, the moral is pointed straight out to the audience at the end of the play.

Producing the play

The best way of performing *The Trial of Trimmer Trend* successfully is to study the principles of morality plays discussed in this introduction. The production should be stylized, with appropriate colours and costumes. Performances of stereotypes require certain mannerisms and attitudes: they are larger-than-life characters. MR TREND can be played straight (but with good comic timing) and his conscience should be played sympatheti-

cally. The CONSCIENCE is really the hero of the play. The NAR-
RATOR should roll out his words dramatically, like the Master of
Ceremonies in television's *Good Old Days*. The audience should
be freely encouraged to hiss, boo and cheer, as they would do in
a pantomime. Props should be brightly coloured, perhaps in cartoon style, following pantomime tradition. A good pianist should
work with the actors to produce dramatic chords, sinister trembles, sad music, as appropriate. This musical accompaniment is an
essential part of the melodramatic style. The whole production
should be very colourful, highly stylized, fast and – one hopes –
very entertaining. The basic script will not survive any attempt to
make the play realistic or subtle. The bolder the images, the
clearer the teaching.

Venues

Before staging a street theatre production, several things
should be borne in mind. Most street theatre venues – parks, market places, city squares – attract a fluctuating audience. A play, as
opposed to a series of sketches, needs an audience prepared to
stay for the duration of the performance. The best way of ensuring
this is to choose a secluded venue, such as the enclosed courtyard
where the play was first performed ; then to advertise the performance through the streets of the city. Literature should give
details of the length of the play, as well as clearly stating that it is
free! Music is a vital ingredient in street theatre: it may be impossible to wheel on an old honky-tonk piano (although we did for
the first production) so a variety of instruments can be used.

Most groups will probably want to perform the play indoors, in
which case lights and sets can be used. Dramatic silhouettes, stage
fights and deathbed scenes with subdued lighting will bring the
play more obviously into the context of Victorian melodrama.

Casting

The first amateur production by Breadrock seemed to involve a
cast of thousands. Actually, it was about twenty-five. This should
not deter smaller groups. Riding Lights Theatre Company staged
The Trial of Trimmer Trend professionally in 1977, at St Andrew's
Undershaft Centre in London, using a cast of six. The doublings
were made possible by extensive use of masks, which were hung
on a bright green hatstand. The hatstand was the centrepiece of
the set, and later became the focus for the crucifixion. Each actor
picked up a mask, as required, and became the appropriate
character. Eventually, all the masks, as well as the sacks of guilt
carried by Conscience, were hung on the figure of Christ, who was

crucified on the hatstand This approach enhanced the stylization of the play.

Approaches to the production will vary according to the number of people and the nature of the talent available. Most amateur groups admit to a reasonable percentage of 'coarse actors' in their midst (see *The Art of Coarse Acting* by Michael Green). *The Trial of Trimmer Trend* is not exactly ham actor-proof, but it is intended to survive the occasional bit-part player who waves his arms like a marionette every time he speaks or the unemployed operatic singer who takes ten minutes to die. A defect in one context can be an advantage in another; even the worst performance may accidentally add to the quality of the melodrama. This being said, there is no need to convince ourselves further that the excesses of church drama groups will actually improve the production. To play melodrama well requires flair. If the talent is found in one sex rather than the other, roles can be reversed, although it is probably best to keep the Trend family as it is. Dr Glossover Thinly, for instance, has been successfully played as a female American psychiatrist. Many interpretations are possible, even within the narrow confines of stereotypes and symbolic characters.

Costumes

Costumes should reflect the symbolism in the play, wherever possible (see the reference to *The Castell of Perseverance* on pages 88–89). The EXECUTIONER represents Death; his costume can imitate the skeletal figure of the medieval plays, or the hangman of recent times, with his noose and black hood. TRIMMER TREND'S costume should typify the trendy executive; whilst his CONSCIENCE needs a more cartoon approach: he is a clown-like figure and can wear a white face; or a costume, all in white, which reflects every detail of Mr Trend's executive suit. CONSCIENCE carries large sacks, marked 'Guilt', hanging round his neck. DIVORCE, as a false conscience to Mr Trend, should have a similar costume to CONSCIENCE, but in a vivid colour. GENERAL CONFORMITY needs a military uniform (which can be designed specially). The ARMY OF APATHY should be sloppily dressed; it is not essential for the recruits to wear the same clothes, but their attitudes, movements and vacant stares should be identical. The DOCTOR is a friendly G.P., who carries an old, black bag; he is modelled on the typical, gruff, good-hearted type, wearing a baggy suit and stethoscope round his neck, familiar from many TV programmes (for those who remember, the archetype was Dr Cameron, played by Andrew Cruickshank). The AUTHOR, at the end of the play, must carry a label, or wear a T-shirt, clearly

marked 'Author'. Finally, the NARRATOR, as a master of ceremonies at the music hall, should wear a top hat, black cape, white
gloves, and carry a cane. Other costumes can be deduced from the
name and the context of the character.

The Trial of Trimmer Trend
A Morality Play
by Murray Watts

CAST

NARRATOR
GUARD ONE
GUARD TWO
EXECUTIONER
TRIMMER TREND
CONSCIENCE
SIMON SLIGHT-OVERSIGHT
TONGUELY SMOOTHCHEEK
DOCTOR
FIDELITY TREND
DOWNHILL TREND
DIVORCE
MORALITY SLIPPING
DOCTOR GLOSSOVER THINLY
GENERAL CONFORMITY
ARMY OF APATHY
JUDGE
CLERK OF COURT
FOREMAN OF THE JURY
JURY
MILES MISSPOINT
AUTHOR

Scene One

(*Enter* MR TREND *between armed guards, handcuffed. They halt before the* EXECUTIONER. NARRATOR *steps forward*)

NARRATOR: Behold the devilish dilemma of Mr Trend! (*Drums*) Descry his dark, desperate and damnable plight! (*Drums*) Despise his despicable and deleterious deeds, dastardly decimations and declivitous downfall! (*Drums*) Disembogue your disapproval at the distinct divagations of one who – crass criminal – connived to concuss and confute his comminating conscience!! (*Drums*) His pure, innocent and serviceable conscience, cruelly beaten, silenced and ignored! (*Drums*) Now he faces his doom. (*Drums*) Who will plead for him? Who will rescue him? (*Drums*) Let us, the players, engage your eager attention in ennucleating the events for your encephalic edification, up to and including the tragical court case of *Trimmer* Trend!! (*Final drum roll.* NARRATOR *produces a sign: '10 YRS AGO'. Exeunt*)

Scene Two – Mr Trend's office

(*Enter* TREND *and* CONSCIENCE *carrying several sacks. They are arguing*)

TREND: For the last time, will you shut up?

CONSCIENCE: I'm only doing my job.

TREND: Well, will you go and do your job somewhere nice and quiet, please, where I can't hear you.

CONSCIENCE: You don't seem to understand, I am your *conscience*, Mr Trend.

TREND: As you have said before. Now run along, there's a good conscience.

CONSCIENCE: I'm not a good conscience, that's just the trouble. Look at this. (*Shows heavy sack marked 'Guilt'*) I've had to carry this around with me for the last year and a half, ever since that shady business deal of yours with

Sham Enterprises PLC It's more than I can take.

TREND: I'd quite forgotten about that, Conscience, yes, I must do something about that. Sometime, sooner or later, I must do something about that ...

CONSCIENCE: Today? Now? Please? It's terribly heavy, you know. (*Enter* SIMON SLIGHT-OVERSIGHT, *the boss, conveniently distracting* TREND, *who pushes* CONSCIENCE *aside*)

TREND: Ah, good morning sir, I was just about to pick up the phone and ring you --

CONSCIENCE: Rubbi— (TREND *stifles him*)

TREND: Just on the point of it.

OVERSIGHT: Good, because I need to know immediately about the contract – has it been signed?

TREND: Um – er .. has it been signed? .. er, which one, sir?

OVERSIGHT: With the Machine Appliance Co., *the contract*, Mr Trend, that we urgently need ..

TREND: Yes, yes, *the contract*. Excuse me, may I just ring one of my consultants a moment? Hello, Rent-an-Excuse, could you help me? I'm in a spot of bother here.

OVERSIGHT: The contract, Mr Trend.

TREND: (*Pause*) It's been signed. (*Shout from* CONSCIENCE)

OVERSIGHT: What's that noise?

TREND: Noise? I don't hear any noise (*Enter* TONGUELY SMOOTHCHEEK) AAH! Tonguely Smoothcheek, so glad you could come, I was just telling Mr Slight-Oversight that I had, in fact, signed the contract and he was about to ask me why there had been such a delay.

SMOOTHCHEEK: Delay? Mr Oversight, surely there must be some misunderstanding, why, I saw a letter on this desk on Thursday morning confirming the arrangement. (CONSCIENCE *cries out in protest*) I'm sorry, did somebody say something? *And*, I might add, there has been a personal phone call to the firm congratulating us on our speed of delivery.

OVERSIGHT: You mean, all the material has been delivered?

SMOOTHCHEEK: It's on its way right now.

OVERSIGHT: Has it arrived yet?

CONSCIENCE: No, it hasn't even been sent!

TREND: (*Hastily*) Traffic jams, sir …

SMOOTHCHEEK: Yes, sir, on the news this morning, diversions on the A62, widespread delays …

OVERSIGHT: Still, we're in the clear as far as our guaranteed date of delivery is concerned?

TREND: I'd say we were all in the clear, sir.

CONSCIENCE: I'd say we were all in a mess. (TREND *coughs loudly*)

OVERSIGHT: Did you say something about a mess, Mr Trend?

TREND: Mess? I should hope not, Mr Oversight, I pride myself on keeping everything out in the open (*he pushes* CONSCIENCE *under the desk*) and if there was any kind of mess up, you'd be the first to know.

OVERSIGHT: Good. Well done, men – I knew I could count on you. (*Exit*)

SMOOTHCHEEK: I'd do something about that cough if I were you, Mr Trend.

TREND: Yes, er, I must do something about that cough, you're right – and thanks for your help.

SMOOTHCHEEK: That's O.K. Here's my card. Always at your service. Only I should get something done about that cough. (*Exit*)

TREND: He's right, very nasty things, coughs.

CONSCIENCE: (*Emerging*) Talking about nasty things, look at this. (*Points to a new sack, marked 'Guilt'*) All that in five minutes – lies, double-dealing –

TREND: (*Business-like*) Excuse me, I'm very busy, would you mind?

CONSCIENCE: Why do I have to be your conscience? Why can't I be someone else's conscience? I'm like a pack horse. I ought to resign, you know, but I can't. Look – (*pointing to old sack*) you still haven't done anything about that last lot of dishonest dealings with Sham Enterprises.

TREND: I am very busy this morning. I certainly intend to clear things up as soon as possible, but please leave me alone.

CONSCIENCE: No, no, no! I demand fair play for consciences!

Rights for consciences! (*Brings out a placard*) Votes for consciences!

TREND: My dear Conscience (*taking out a mallet*) how often have I told you not to bother me at work? (*Hits him on the head. Exit*)

Scene Three

(*Enter* DOCTOR, *carrying a black case, marked 'Royal Society for the Prevention of Cruelty to Consciences'*)

DOCTOR: What's this? A conscience falling unconscious through over conscientiousness? Obviously a critical case. How does it feel?

CONSCIENCE: (*Stirring*) It feels as if I've been hit just here with a mallet.

DOCTOR: Yes, (*inspecting mallet*) there's been a nasty outbreak of mallets hitting consciences recently. (*Looks in his case*) Anti-mallet pills ... anti-infection ... anti-biotic ... antidote ... anti-Doris ... no anti-mallet pills, I'm afraid, but have you tried wearing one of these? (*Produces steel hat*)

CONSCIENCE: Ah. No, not allowed, I'm sorry to say. I have orders to stay as sensitive as I can, no hats, no suits of armour ... however, I am becoming rapidly hardened to the outside world.

DOCTOR: A hardened conscience! Do you realise, that can be absolutely fatal?

CONSCIENCE: I do, I do, but how else can I manage to carry all this around as well as putting up with mallets, and sledgehammers, not to mention pick-axes?

DOCTOR: Let me listen to your heart. Stuttering stethoscopes! Thundering thermometers! Noxious National Health Services! This heart is in an extreme state of hardening! That could lead to –

CONSCIENCE: Lack of love in the home!

DOCTOR: Callous indifference to other people – wives – children!

CONSCIENCE: Eventual break-up of a marriage!

DOCTOR: All because so much of this has accumulated (*shows sacks*) that it has become too much for one conscience to bear, and so conscience ceases to operate even on the most crucial occasions. Quick, there's no time to lose – go home immediately – before it's too late – patch up relationships – get him to apologise – to ask for forgiveness – to make a new start. Hurry! Run! (CONSCIENCE *struggles off*)

NARRATOR: Hurry! Faster! Faster! See how our hero runs to ruefully remonstrate over the rampant rot now reaching the roots of relationships in the home of Mr Trend. Alas! Alack! Woe! Disaster upon disaster! Divorce dons his devilish disguise, collaborating to compound the cataclysmic cruelty to an increasingly cataleptic conscience. (*Exit* NARRATOR, *as* DIVORCE *hides under the table*)

Scene Four – Mr Trend's home

(MR TREND *is packing his suitcase*)

FIDELITY: You promised.

TREND: What?

FIDELITY: In church, you promised!

TREND: Church … now let me see, when did I last go there?

FIDELITY: Your wedding.

TREND: My wedding. Yes, and a few harvest festivals, of course. Christmas, Easter, a Sunday School pageant. Not bad.

FIDELITY: Never mind about them. *Our wedding, you promised.*

TREND: I promised never to leave you, is that what you're trying to tell me? For better or for worse, for richer or for poorer, etc. etc.?

FIDELITY: I've never stopped loving you.

TREND: (*Nonplussed for a moment*) Don't worry. I'll be back … I just need a little space, once in a while. Room for manoeuvre … That's what love is all about.

FIDELITY: *I* need love. Your daughter needs love.

TREND: Um … I wonder if the 6.10 goes all the way to Blackheath or if it stops off at Lewisham?

FIDELITY: (*Despairing*) Go on then, get out.

TREND: I'm going. (*He picks up his bags and begins to leave*)

FIDELITY: (*Running and making a final effort*) But why? This is your home, your family. (*Pause*) Why are you just – going?

TREND: I'm going because you've just told me to get out.

FIDELITY: I told you to *get out* because you're *going*!

TREND: Well then, let's just say that I'm going.
(*Enter* CONSCIENCE *struggling, out of breath*)

CONSCIENCE: No, no, back, this instant, you're not going, sit down, think – *think*.

TREND: But I don't want to think! I want to act completely on the spur of the moment!

CONSCIENCE: Think of your daughter.

TREND: No, I don't want to think about her.

CONSCIENCE: Your daughter. (*Enter* DOWNHILL, *outrageously dressed*) Downhill Trend.

TREND: She's a delinquent.

CONSCIENCE: She's a delinquent, he says, and why is she a delinquent, Mr Trend? Why?

TREND: Leave me alone.

CONSCIENCE: No, speak to her.

TREND: I'm sorry … look … I'll … I'll write you a letter.

CONSCIENCE: A letter! That's what you offer in exchange for being a father to her. It's going to have to be a mighty good letter!

TREND: I'll visit you.

CONSCIENCE: It's not enough.

TREND: Silence! I am following my conscience in this matter!

CONSCIENCE: You must be joking. I'm your conscience.

TREND: This is my conscience. (DIVORCE *gets out, wearing the label: 'Conscience'*)

DIVORCE: Pleased to make your acquaintance, I'm sure. Mr Trend and I have discussed this matter in some depth and we both agree that a rift in a marriage is tragic. Perhaps the most tragic thing of all. Tragic, but necessary, in *some* cases – but maybe only for a time – maybe just till we get our perspective back? Right, Mr Trend?

TREND: Right.

CONSCIENCE: Wrong.

TREND: Don't interrupt! (*He hits him on the head*) Now, you were saying?

DIVORCE: Yes, maybe only a few days, a week or two – a trial separation, and we are not, quite definitely not, talking of divorce here.

TREND: (*To* FIDELITY) You see, I'm not divorcing

you, no … I just need time … time to think …

DIVORCE: To come back to a stronger relationship.

TREND: Yes, to come back to a stronger relationship.

FIDELITY: There's someone else.

DIVORCE: No.

TREND: No. Definitely, that has nothing to do with it. (*Enter* MORALITY SLIPPING)

CONSCIENCE: Morality Slipping has nothing to do with it? (*He shows her to him*)

TREND: Well …

FIDELITY: Well?

CONSCIENCE: Well??

DIVORCE: (*Fighting hard*) Um … she is only a symptom of the breakdown that already existed …

TREND: Um … only a symptom of the breakdown that already existed …

FIDELITY: Don't give me that … stuff!

CONSCIENCE: Exactly. Look at it for what it is. (*He reveals the two labels on them: 'Divorce' and 'Adultery'*. DIVORCE *cowers on the floor.* MR TREND *is at a moment of crisis.* CONSCIENCE *continues*)

CONSCIENCE: Now look at your family … wife …

FIDELITY: Why? Why this?

CONSCIENCE: And daughter …

DOWNHILL: It's all right, Dad, you go ahead. Why should I care what you do? You never cared what I did. Leave us. Please yourself, like you always did.

TREND: No, it wasn't like that. Remember all those toys you had … I gave you?

DOWNHILL: Big presents! That's what you were, Father Christmas! Here, have a present, have a present, and don't look too hard in case you see Daddy jumping into bed with somebody else's Mummy!

CONSCIENCE: It's not too late. It's not too late. Never too late – to make amends. Forgiveness. A new start. Yes. Today … (DIVORCE *leaps up*)

DIVORCE: Forgiveness, what's that got to do with it?

CONSCIENCE: A lot. (DIVORCE *throws him to the ground. Drumbeats, sound effects, during the stage fight*)

DIVORCE: Religion is ideals. What about real life? (CONSCIENCE *struggles up*)

CONSCIENCE: Real life … so you think you're more real than marriage?

DIVORCE: Let's see. (*They fight*) Religion, that's all you are, religion in disguise.

CONSCIENCE: In that case, everybody's religious. Everybody. We all have a conscience. We all know more about right and wrong than we admit. (*They continue fighting*)

DIVORCE: No, it all boils down to self. There's no right or wrong. (*He has won the fight.* CONSCIENCE *has collapsed at the feet of* FIDELITY *and* DOWNHILL) You just have to do what you have to do.

TREND: I'm sorry. I'm just doing what I have to do. Goodbye. (*Exeunt* TREND, DIVORCE *and* MORALITY SLIPPING *stage left and* FIDELITY *and* DOWNHILL *stage right. Sad music as* NARRATOR *enters and attaches another sack of 'Guilt' to* CONSCIENCE, *who crawls off*)

Scene Five – A penthouse flat

NARRATOR: Five years later the fatal flaw of Mr Trend fructifies in a Freudian fricassée of super-subtle self-deceptions! See at last how he is forced by expert advice to moorishly murder his mouldering mentor … !! (*Enter* MORALITY SLIPPING, *bringing tea to* TREND)

MORALITY: How was work today, darling?

TREND: Oh, we got in a bit of a flap about some deal or other, but I found a way out.

MORALITY: (*Playfully undoing his shirt button*) You're very good at finding your way out of things, sweetheart.

TREND: Am I really? Oh, thank you.

MORALITY: I don't know what they'd do without you.

TREND: No. I don't know what they'd do without me, to be quite frank. Somebody has to do the dirty work for them. It's chaps like me that make the world go round.

MORALITY: (*Pouring tea*) What I like about you is that you're so cool, nobody can ever get you worked up about anything.

TREND: Well, it's important to keep your cool in the world today, you know, you can't have people panicking all over the place –

(CONSCIENCE *appears behind him, utterly gruesome, laden with sacks*) aaaaaaaaghh!!

MORALITY: Darling, are you all right?

TREND: Yes! No! Um. No. Yes. Yes ... Yes. I just forgot something that I remembered. I mean it's all right. I've just lost something.

MORALITY: What?

TREND: My cool. No. My conscience.

MORALITY: Conscience?

TREND: No, don't mention that word, conscious*ness*.

MORALITY: You lost consciousness.

TREND: Yes. Briefly. Blackout. Er ... strain of conscience. WORK. Overwork.

MORALITY: What are you talking about?

TREND: That's it!

MORALITY: What?

TREND: Nothing!

MORALITY: Nothing?

TREND: Nothing has happened whatsoever.

MORALITY: That's all right then.

TREND: Yes, now I feel perfectly all right. (CONSCIENCE *pops up again*) – aaaaarghh!! Get that coshnunsh out of here!

MORALITY: Coshnunsh?

TREND: Coshnunsh, what are you talking about? Aaargh!

MORALITY: (*Phoning*) Hello, Dr Thinly? He's having another attack. Delirious. Could you possibly see him? It's urgent! (*Puts phone down*) I'll take you to his surgery at once.

CONSCIENCE: (*To* TREND) *I* need a doctor! Get *me* the doctor! I'm dying, you know, I'm at death's door. I need someone to get rid of all this, help me!

TREND: (*Leaving*) I need someone to get rid of you!

MORALITY: Dr Glossover Thinly will solve everything. (*She helps him out*)

Scene Six – Dr Glossover's surgery

(MR TREND *lies on the psychiatrist's couch*, CONSCIENCE *lies on the floor*)

GLOSSOVER: Now, what can I do ... away with ... for you?

TREND: I've got a severe pain in my conscience.

GLOSSOVER: (*Writing*) Severe pain in ... conscience. How long have you had this?

TREND: Since my childhood ... it started ... at school ... or even before ... I remember ... I copied something from someone in an exam ...

CONSCIENCE: Cheated.

GLOSSOVER: You received assistance from a friend ... in an exam.

TREND: I felt remorse.

GLOSSOVER: That's serious. Remorse.

TREND: I took one or two things ... little things ... took ...

CONSCIENCE: Stole ...

GLOSSOVER: Borrowed some things.

TREND: I meant to give them back, of course.

GLOSSOVER: Gave them back, of course.

TREND: Then I was dishonest ... told a few ...

CONSCIENCE: Lies.

GLOSSOVER: Lies?

TREND: White lies.

GLOSSOVER: A few half-truths.

TREND: Nothing serious.

GLOSSOVER: And yet you had this pain in your conscience?

TREND: Yes, it began to grow ... all night parties ... just a few ... I got drunk and slept with my girl-friend ... I felt it was ... not right, somehow ... somehow, the day after ... we both felt ...

CONSCIENCE: *Guilty.*

GLOSSOVER: *Please.* Do not mention that word. I could be struck off the register, d'you hear? Good. Now. You experimented with sex ...

TREND: My conscience troubled me ...

GLOSSOVER: Troubled you about something beautiful, good and healthy?

TREND: No. Troubled me because it didn't turn out that way ... because there was no love ...

GLOSSOVER: Deprived childhood.

TREND: No! (CONSCIENCE *is impressed*) Not more than anyone else, I wasn't a deprived child. It was I who deprived ... others. (CONSCIENCE *shakes his hand*) That was it ... at work, at home, friendships ... no ... love ... I kept it all for myself ...

GLOSSOVER: How long have you had this?

TREND: The pain?

GLOSSOVER: No, the conscience.

TREND: Seems like a lifetime

GLOSSOVER: You are seriously ill. You are suffering from sado-masochistic-paranoid-schizophrenia, and every kind of fixation under the sun. This conscience you refer to (*advancing on* CONSCIENCE) is a figment of your imagination.

CONSCIENCE: No. I'm real, I'm real!

GLOSSOVER: A nightmare ...

CONSCIENCE: Look, it's me!

TREND: (*Looking*) Aaaaarghh!!

GLOSSOVER: A perversion of the true, free ... *you* ... freedom ... truth ...

TREND: I want freedom.

GLOSSOVER: You shall have freedom. (*Pause*) For only five pounds. This book: *The Fight For Freedom* shall give you freedom! Sign here. (DOCTOR *leaps through the window*)

DOCTOR: Hold it! Don't sign! That book is a notorious manual on how to murder your conscience!

TREND: How?

DOCTOR: Pretence! Persuasion! Glossing over glaring faults! Calling guilt – maturity and experience! Calling sin – self-discovery!

GLOSSOVER: *Sin!* How dare you utter such blasphemy – that word has caused more damage than any other in the whole history of mankind. I'm having it erased from the dictionary. Sign here.

DOCTOR: Wait. There is another book. (*He produces a large book marked 'Bible'*) Only this one will not *comfort* your conscience; it will hurt cruelly; it will convict your conscience ... of sin. *But* ... it will show you the way to get rid of all sin ... for ever.

TREND: (*Reads*) The Bible.

GLOSSOVER: (*Snatching it away*) You poor, pathetic, medieval-minded fool. Do I have to drag you screaming into the twentieth century?

DOCTOR: Don't listen. There is nothing modern about his attitude to sin. It's as old as Satan. (TREND *weighs up the books*) The choice is yours.

GLOSSOVER: Choose now!

DOCTOR: Choose wisely! (*Exeunt* DOCTORS, TREND *and* CONSCIENCE)

Scene Seven – A street

(TREND *looks at the books: first, the Bible*)

CONSCIENCE: I feel the blood coming back into my veins ... that's better ... that's better ... I can breathe .. but now I feel the weight of all this guilt ... (TREND *slams the Bible shut and opens the other book*) I feel numb, the strength is going from me ... I ... Where am I ... I feel like falling asleep ... it's nice .. but ... I can't breathe ... (TREND *reopens Bible*) Ah ... ah ... I'm breathing ... deeply ... (*There is a sound of marching*)

TREND: Marching? An army? (*Enter* GENERAL CONFORMITY *and* TROOPS)

CONFORMITY: Hep-by, hep-by, hep-by, hep-by, hep-by, squad will turn to the right in threes, to the right, turn, squad will turn on their television sets, to the left, switch, squad will watch what everybody else watches, eyes front. Now get watching, you miserable lot of nonconformists.

TREND: Who are you?

CONFORMITY: General Conformity, laddie, and stand with your hands in your pockets and your eyes glazed when you're talking to me. Drop that jaw. I should hope so. And let's have none of this making serious decisions during a routine drill. Whatsyername?

TREND: Trend, sir.

CONFORMITY: Private Trend. I see. Squad, shun! Squad slope downhill in all matters of personal morality, squad, stand at ease when facing important decisions. Stand easy! And do nothing about anything. Private Trend, fall in!

TREND: But – but – my conscience.

CONFORMITY: Private Trend, stand stock still! Squad! Squad re-tire one pace. Stand at ease! (TREND *finds himself in the army by doing nothing*)

TREND: I feel I ought to ... go ... my own way ... do what I think ... follow my conscience.

CONFORMITY: YOU PATHETIC LITTLE MUMMY'S BOY OF A RELIGIOUS NUTCASE!! 'Ello, 'ello, what's this what's this? (*Picking* up *Bible*) *The*-Bible. Oh dear, oh dear, you've got it coming to you, laddie, you can be sentenced to up to two hours' public embarrassment, for reading a book like this … if your friends were to find out, laddie …

TREND: Yessir.

CONFORMITY: From now on you will not read this book, laddie.

TREND: Nossir.

CONFORMITY: Why will you not read this book, laddie?

TREND: Don't know, sir.

CONFORMITY: Well done, private Trend, well done. You don't know why you will not read this book, laddie?

TREND: Nossir.

CONFORMITY: Because nobody else does, they just don't, laddie. Is that clear?

TREND: Right, sir.

CONFORMITY: Right. SQUAD WILL FOLLOW THE FASHION.

SQUAD: SAH!

CONFORMITY: SQUAD WILL BELIEVE WHAT THE EXPERTS TELL THEM.

SQUAD: SAH!

CONFORMITY: SQUAD WILL NOT INVESTIGATE FOR THEMSELVES.

SQUAD: SAH!

CONFORMITY: (*To* TREND) Don't let me catch you stepping out of line again or you'll be thoroughly ridiculed, is that clear, number 892?

TREND: SAH!

CONFORMITY: And wipe that look of rapt attention off your face when you're talking to me. Next time I expect to see a marked decrease of interest and a pretty good display of apathy. SQUAD, APATHETICALLY, MARCH. (*They leave*) Let's have more conformity there … I want a lot less personality in this squad … (*Exeunt. Enter* NARRATOR *who observes rejection of the Bible*)

NARRATOR: Alas! Woe! Miserere mei! Horrible Holocaust! Ineffably felonious fiend! Ah me! The end is near! The cruel catharsis comes! The catastrophic catastasis commences! Hoodwinked by hideous devices,

Mr Trend succumbs to the prevailing wind of fashion powerfully propelled by the malicious magnate General Conformity and his squad of pathetic time-serving parasites – he abandons hope – (TREND *puts down the Bible*) and thus deals the fatal, fulgorous, finishing blow to   CONSCIENCE!!

Scene Eight · The same place

CONSCIENCE   Have mercy on me   pity me ... aaah

TREND: (*Reading* GLOSSOVER'S *book*) Sin is a delusion of the diseased mind. It is not true to say that there is a right or wrong

CONSCIENCE   Aaah'

TREND: It may well depend on the individual situation.

CONSCIENCE: Help me

TREND: Religion exaggerates guilt, causing excessive soul-searching ... the remedy is to see God in everyone, especially in yourself ...

CONSCIENCE.   Mercy!

TREND.   Realise your own potential ...

CONSCIENCE: Aaaaagh ...

TREND   Do not be dominated by your conscience . Learn to quell and control, and if necessary, reject, the promptings of your conscience ..

CONSCIENCE: Aaaah! ... I die! Pity my agony, aah, sweet world, farewell, sun, moon ... (TREND *finishes him off by clubbing him on the head*)

TREND: Phew! Now I can really start living! Whoopee! (GUARD ONE *and* GUARD TWO *appear, followed by* DOCTOR)

GUARD ONE: Halt! In the name of the law!

TREND: Law? What law!

GUARD TWO'   Trimmer Try-it-on Trend?

TREND.   Yes?

GUARD TWO: You are under arrest.

TREND   Arrest? But – but –

GUARD ONE   You are charged with gross neglect of your moral duty.

TREND: What the –

GUARD TWO: You are charged with grievous evasion of conscience, with intent to please yourself and live your own life in total disregard for others

GUARD ONE: You are charged with neglect, malnutrition and assault of your conscience and with – Doctor? (DOCTOR *has been examining* CONSCIENCE)

DOCTOR: Yes, I'm afraid so –

GUARD ONE: The murder of the said Conscience. (*Dramatic chord on piano*)

TREND: Murder ... ?? I ... I ... Please ... my solicitor ...

GUARD TWO: You are to appear forthwith before the Lord Chief Justice at the Great Assize.

GUARD ONE: March.

TREND: I can explain ... (*Exeunt*)

NARRATOR: Behold the devilish dilemma of Mr Trend! (*Drums*) Descry his dark, desperate and damnable plight! (*Drums*) Despise his despicable and deleterious deeds, dastardly decimations and declivitous downfall! (*Drums*) The plot has come full circle! Behold the judge, jury, evidence, and executioner! Silence in court!!

Scene Nine – The courtroom

(*They take up positions.* CONSCIENCE *is evidence on a stretcher marked 'Exhibit A'. The* DOCTOR *dons a wig and gown, becoming Counsel for the Prosecution*)

JUDGE: You are accused of murdering your conscience. Do you have anything to say?

TREND: Yes, your Honour, I can explain. Please ...

CLERK: Does the defendant wish to undertake his own defence?

JUDGE: Mr Trend?

TREND: Yes, m'Lud. Please call the first witness. (*Enter* TONGUELY SMOOTHCHEEK)

CLERK: Mr Smoothcheek, place your hand on the Bible. Do you promise to tell the truth, the whole truth, and nothing but the truth?

SMOOTHCHEEK: I promise to tell the truth, the whole truth, and nothing but the truth, so help me God, and believe me, I've always been very religious, very, went to church every Sunday, regular as clockwork, but when it comes to Mr Trend, a man of integrity, a man of his word – m'Lud, gentlemen of the jury –

never, I would repeat, never, would he have
down what he's done had he known what he
was doing ... like I do, brought up *religious*
... like .. no ... Ignorance is the problem,
m'Lud .. lack of religious instruction ...

DOCTOR: Objection, m'Lud.

JUDGE: Objection granted.

DOCTOR: *'Ignorantia legis neminem excusat.'* Ignorance of the law is no excuse. Romans one
verse nineteen. (*He picks up the Bible*)
'What can be known about God is plain to all
men, because God has shown it to them.
Ever since the creation of the world his
invisible nature, namely, his eternal power
and deity, has been clearly perceived in the
things that have been made. *So they are
without excuse.'* (*Hands the book back*)

SMOOTHCHEEK: Aaah! .. This book is burning in my hands.
m'Lud .. help ... fire ... (*Exit*)

TREND: Call the next witness, General Conformity
... quick ... he'll explain in no time ...

CLERK: Do you promise to tell the truth, the whole
truth and nothing but the truth?

CONFORMITY: I promise to say anything that doesn't depart
from popular opinion, and if that happens to
be the truth, bally good show, and if not,
bally bad luck, what? So help me, God.
Whatever you conceive him to be. Amen.

TREND: General Conformity, is it true that majority
opinion is in my favour?

CONFORMITY: No doubt about that. None whatever. Social
surveys, gallup polls, TV documentaries,
they're all in your favour, laddie. You are in
the broad stream and brotherhood of mankind.

DOCTOR: Objection, m'Lud.

JUDGE: Objection granted.

DOCTOR: The majority opinion is an unacceptable
defence in this court. Matthew seven verse
thirteen. (*Picks up Bible*) 'The gate is wide
and the way is easy that leads to destruction
and those who enter it are many. The gate is
narrow and the way is hard that leads to life
and those who find it are few!' (*Hands book
back*)

CONFORMITY: This book is burning ... Like a great light ...
I can't see a bally thing ... Blind. I've gone
blind ... Ah! (*Bumps into* CLERK) Show me
the way out, Nincompoop ... (*Exit*)

TREND: Call the next witness ... Doctor Glossover V.
Thinly ... m'Lud ... gentlemen of the jury,
you can depend on him ... he will explain
everything perfectly clearly.

CLERK: Do you promise to tell the truth, the whole
truth and nothing but the truth?

GLOSSOVER: (*Holding Bible*) I promise to tell the truth,
the whole truth ... and ... ah! (*Drops Bible
like hot plate*) Excuse me, I think I'll use this
one if you don't mind. (*Takes out his own
book*) I promise to tell everyone my inner
personality, struggling to emerge through
the aeons of time, the whole me, the real me,
and nothing but a load of rubbish. I'm sorry.
That's odd. I didn't write that. Anyway,
press on. So help myself, amen, and the rest
of it.

TREND: Doctor Glossover.

GLOSSOVER: Yes?

TREND: I am accused of murder.

GLOSSOVER: Ah. Murder, yes. But what do we mean by
murder?

TREND: Sin ... I am accused of sin ... sin ... Help me,
Dr Glossover ... Please ... Tell them I'm a
good chap ... No worse than the next man ...
I'm not a sinner ...

GLOSSOVER: Sin ... sinner ... well, there we are, we *are*
enjoying an antiquarian discussion, aren't
we? Bit like TV's 'Antiques Roadshow' with
all those bits of old furniture turning up. I
think it's about time we all did some furniture
removal. Removed this concept of sin. Let
me read you a passage from my book. Here
it is. 1 John, chapter one, verse eight ...
That's odd ... I don't remember putting that
at the top of the chapter ... Press on anyway.
Sin. 'If we say we have no sin, we deceive
ourselves and the truth is not in us.' Ah ... ah
... Ha! Ha! My mind ... what's happening ...
noises, colours, pink elephants ... good day,
good morning, banana custard to you too,

DOCTOR:
    Madam .. Yes .. (*Exit, mad*)
    'Claiming to be wise they became fools'
    Romans chapter one, verse twenty-two.

JUDGE:
    Counsel for the Prosecution, do you wish to
    call anyone to the witness box?

DOCTOR:
    Yes, m'Lud, but not to question them ..
    merely to show them to the court .. a wife, a
    daughter .. a respected colleague at business
    .. (*Enter* FIDELITY, DOWNHILL, SLIGHT-
    OVERSIGHT) Only three of all the possible
    casualties .. tricked, cozened, lied to,
    deserted .. and neglected ... and a
    conscience ... (*removes blanket*) foully
    murdered! Romans chapter six, verse
    twenty-three: 'The wages of sin is death.'

JUDGE:
    Gentlemen of the jury, what is your verdict?
    (*They consult*)

TREND:
    Your honour, the sight of those people, my
    wife .. my daughter ... those I've wounded
    .. I .. m'Lud ... Mercy ..

FOREMAN:
    As foreman of this jury I pronounce our
    verdict. GUILTY!! (*Commotion in the
    court*)

JUDGE:
    The court will adjourn. (*Exeunt*)

DOCTOR:
    You know what that means .. the black cap.
    (*Exit*)

Scene Ten

    (*The* GUARDS *stand outside the doors of the
    courtroom.* TRIMMER *is left alone*)

TREND:
    Death ... help me. (*Enter* MILES MISSPOINT
    holding a microphone)

MISSPOINT:
    Hello and welcome. It's been a sultry day at
    the Great Assize with the usual crop of
    capital offenders, but perhaps the most
    spine-chilling of all has been the trial of a
    convicted murderer, Trimmer Try-it-on
    Trend. What do you feel now that the court
    case is over?

TREND:
    Help me .. Somebody ...

MISSPOINT:
    Well, there you have it, a desperate and in
    many ways a heart-rendingly forlorn situa-
    tion.

TREND:
    (*Imploring*) Please? Help me!

MISSPOINT:
    I'm sorry .. Excuse me. you're treading on

my lead, thank you … so, with a matter of
minutes rather than hours till the carriage of
justice, in this case execution, which we'll be
covering live, or dead, in the case of the
victim, I hand you back to the studio. Miles
Misspoint. ITN news. The Great Assize.
(*Exit, to News theme tune*)

TREND: Help me … I'm condemned to death … Oh,
God … this … this book … maybe something
here, some clause, a mitigating circumstance
… (*He picks up the Bible but drops it again*)
It's white hot … I must open it. (*There is a
low sound from* CONSCIENCE) Conscience??
… Not dead? (*Dramatic chord on piano*)
Quick … I must read … (*Reads*) 'The wages
of sin is death …' No hope then … What are
you saying? (CONSCIENCE *stirs and feebly
points a finger at the Bible*) Read on … '*But*
… the free gift of God is eternal life in Christ
Jesus our Lord …'

CONSCIENCE: Where am I?

TREND: Conscience is recovering. Quick … five
minutes before the judge returns. I must
read some more … pray God there'll be
enough time …

The Mime*

(*TRIMMER TREND continues to read. His
attention is fixed on the Bible, whilst*
CONSCIENCE *watches the mime. The* JUDGE
enters. He takes off his wig and gown) And
God loved the world so much that he gave
his only Son that whoever believes in him
should not perish but have eternal life …
(*Turns over pages. The* JUDGE *becomes the*
FIGURE OF CHRIST) He gave his life as a
ransom for many. (CONSCIENCE *is watching
the mime, reviving*) He himself bore our sins
in his body on the tree, that we might die to
sin and live to righteousness. (*The* FIGURE
OF CHRIST *removes all the burdens from*

*Cf *The Light of the World* in *Time To Act* by Paul Burbridge &
Murray Watts (Hodder and Stoughton, 1979)

CONSCIENCE *and takes them himself. He
climbs up the ladder to where the*
EXECUTIONER *stands with a hammer and
nails*) Let us draw near with a true heart in
full assurance of faith, with our hearts sprink-
led clean from an evil conscience . . God
shows his love for us in that while we were
still sinners Christ died for us. (*The* FIGURE
OF CHRIST, *laden with sacks, is crucified*)
and Jesus cried with a loud voice 'It is
finished ... Done .. Accomplished .. ' (*The*
FIGURE *on the cross cries out silently and
dies*) ... and they took him down from the
cross and laid him in the tomb ... (*deposition*)
and on the third day he rose again and he
appeared to Peter and the twelve and then to
more than five hundred disciples at one time
... (*Risen* CHRIST *appears to* CONSCIENCE)
Death is swallowed up in victory ... death
where is your victory, grave where is your
sting? (*The* EXECUTIONER *is vanquished*)
The sting of death is sin, and the power of sin
is the law, but thanks be to God who gives us
the victory through our Lord Jesus Christ . .
To all who received him he gave power to
become children of God ... (*The* FIGURE OF
CHRIST *holds up a scroll*) The wages of sin is
death but the free gift of God is eternal life in
Christ Jesus our Lord. (CONSCIENCE *receives
the scroll. The* FIGURE *goes*) Is it too late?
Lord??

CONSCIENCE· Quick. (CONSCIENCE *hands him the scroll,
then lies on the stretcher*)

Scene Eleven

CLERK· Silence in court!! (TREND *begins to read the
scroll to himself.* JUDGE *puts on black cap*)

JUDGE: For selfishness, heartlessness, lack-of-love,
for neglect, malnutrition, assault and murder
of conscience, I sentence you to ...

TREND: m'Lud ... ? (*Hands him the scroll*)

JUDGE· The prisoner is acquitted. (*Uproar in court*)

VOICES: m'Lud ... Objection, m'Lud ... Justice, we
demand justice . .

JUDGE Objection overruled. This is a reprieve

signed by his majesty the King! 'To the
Bearer, the free gift of eternal life' and
what's more, this man's conscience is in
perfectly good order. (CONSCIENCE *leaps up
from the stretcher to which he had returned
on entry of court. Further uproar*) Let no one
ever bring any accusation against this man
ever again. (*He walks out and all follow
obediently*)

Scene Twelve – A street near the courtroom

(*Enter from one side the* AUTHOR *and from
the other* MILES MISSPOINT)

MISSPOINT: Hey, what time's the execution?

AUTHOR: You're two thousand years too late.

MISSPOINT: Two thousand years too late?!! I've got to
get something done about this watch
(*Enter* CONSCIENCE *and* TREND) No – wait –
it's all right ... there he is. Mr Trend? Could
you spare me a word for the viewers just
before you get executed?

TREND: I'm not getting executed.

MISSPOINT: You're not?

TREND: I'm free.

MISSPOINT: Free?

TREND: Been acquitted.

MISSPOINT: *Acquitted*? You mean no sssst!
Bangbangbang! Ulllkk! (*Imitates slitting
throat, firing squad and hanging*)

TREND: Nope.

MISSPOINT: But what about the News at Ten? We were
devoting the whole of Part Two to that!

TREND: Sorry.

MISSPOINT: Well ... er ... what are you going to do now
... now you're *not* getting ssst!
Bangbangbang! Ullkk!

TREND: Ask my Conscience.

CONSCIENCE: (*Looking up from reading the Bible*) Oh.
well, it says here about repentance and
making amends and asking for people's
forgiveness, forgiving others who have
wronged you, and generally making a new
start.

TREND: So I'll be doing that.

MISSPOINT: That's just great, that is. *Great.* That wouldn't even look interesting in the personal columns of *The Times!* What about the News at Ten?

TREND: Frankly, I couldn't give a damn about – (CONSCIENCE *nudges him*)

CONSCIENCE: Er ... ?

TREND: I mean, I don't think the News at Ten is really the issue here. The issue is that I'm free, and I'm really happy.

CONSCIENCE: Goodbye. (*Exeunt* TREND *and* CONSCIENCE)

MISSPOINT: I'll get the sack for this. I can just see the News Editor! (*Imitating*) No execution, huh? You should have laid *on* an execution, in fact I think I will lay on an execution right now – yours!! (*Begins to cry*)

AUTHOR: Never mind. Why don't you look at this? (*Picks up Bible*) It's the most sensational book that's ever been written.

MISSPOINT: (*Perking up*) The most sensational!!

AUTHOR: The world's number-one bestseller ...

MISSPOINT: Number-one bestseller!! (*Reads*) *Risen* from the *dead* ... You're right, this is sensational ... Hey, why don't I write a story about how Mr Trend faced execution but was dramatically acquitted?

AUTHOR: I'm afraid I've just written one. In fact, this is the end of it.

MISSPOINT: Oh, well, maybe I could make a film of this book ... and call it (*inspired*) *The Greatest Story Ever Told!!*

AUTHOR: It's already been done.

MISSPOINT: Oh, wait!! I've got it ... an incredible idea. I'll get Franco Zeffirelli to direct a film and call it *Jesus of Nazareth!!*

AUTHOR: Could I suggest an alternative?

MISSPOINT: Sure.

AUTHOR: Read it. Read the book yourself.

MISSPOINT: Oh, no ... no ... no ...

AUTHOR: Yes ... Read the Bible.

MISSPOINT: Oh, no, look, I'm just a reporter ... a spectator ... one of the audience ... I don't want to get involved or anything.

AUTHOR: But you can't read this book without getting involved for or against.

MISSPOINT: Oh, now look, I'm here in a strictly professional capacity ... strictly an observer ... one of the audience ... It may be all right for religious nutcases like Mr Trend – (*Enter* MISSPOINT'S CONSCIENCE)

M's CONSCIENCE: I think you ought to read it.

MISSPOINT: You do?

M's CONSCIENCE: Yes. You should stop beating about the bush.

AUTHOR: Who's that?

MISSPOINT: Oh. That's, umm ... (*stifling him*) no one.

DOCTOR: Your conscience, perhaps?

MISSPOINT: No!!

M's CONSCIENCE: Yes!! (MISSPOINT *hits him on the head*)

MISSPOINT: Er, look, I've got to get going. (*To his* CONSCIENCE) How many times have I told you not to bother me at work? (*Exeunt*)

THE END

Rolling In The Aisles

by Murray Watts

'There was a blinding flash of lightning and Emily, aged five, rushed into the house, shouting: "Mummy, Mummy, God has just taken my picture!"'

The wide range of this book makes it more than the traditional collection of religious humour. As well as being highly entertaining, *Rolling In The Aisles* is illuminating, poignant and provocative, a must for speakers searching for the telling anecdote, and a delight to all lovers of the most dangerous kind of humour, the kind that reveals the truth about ourselves.

MURRAY WATTS is a playwright and a founding director of the Riding Lights Theatre Company, award winners at the Edinburgh Fringe Festival and famous for their unique blend of comic and serious material. He is author of several books, including the companion volume *Bats in the Belfry*, and editor of *Laughter in Heaven*.

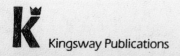

Kingsway Publications

Bats In The Belfry

by Murray Watts

'An atheist was lying in the funeral parlour. The mortician put the finishing touches to the body and sighed, "Look at him—all dressed up and nowhere to go."'

This is religious humour with a difference. Not only is it very funny, but also illuminating and sometimes disturbing—a book to cherish. If you need a story to make a point, a joke or open a speech, or simply something to lift your spirits, the solution is at hand!

MURRAY WATTS is an award-winning playwright, whose work has been performed on stage, TV and radio. He is the author of several books including *Laughter in Heaven* and the bestselling *Rolling in the Aisles*.

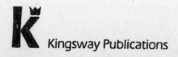

Kingsway Publications